SAMMY:
Child Survivor of the Holocaust

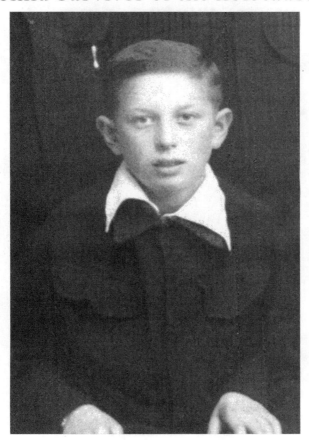

Samuel R. Harris
(Szlamek Rzeznik)

SAMMY:
Child Survivor of the Holocaust

by Samuel R. Harris and Cheryl Gorder

Second Printing

Printing History

Blue Bird Publishing Inc 1999
AH Handy   2005

Library of Congress Control Number
2004093250

ISBN   0-933025-87-4

Cover Art Ruth Perkins
Printed in the United States of America

" I believe that all of us have something tremendously important to learn from his story. The language is clear and simple, and the story of survival against the odds is one that resonates through the ages. On behalf of generations of schoolchildren to come, thank you, Sam Harris, for the gift of this gripping story."—**Dr. Glenn W. McGee**, Illinois State Superintendent of Education.

"This gripping first person account of a child caught in the horror of the Holocaust is a testament to the enduring resilience of faith and the ability of the human spirit to rebound from tremendous adversity. I highly recommend *Sammy: Child Survivor of the Holocaust* to educators who are looking for material that will have impact with middle-age students."—**Dr. Cozette Buckney**, Chief Education Officer, Chicago Public Schools.

"To my knowledge Sam Harris is one of the, if not the, youngest Holocaust survivors who actually spent time in a concentration camp and was miraculously saved. Almost without exception, all Jewish children his age were, after the arrest of their families, immediately murdered. His story is one that should be read by children to learn how a young boy survived the Holocaust. It is a story of hope and courage."—**Ernest W. Michel**, Chairman, World Gathering Jewish Holocaust Survivors, author of *Promises to Keep: One Man's Journey Against Incredible Odds*.

"*Sammy: Child Survivor of the Holocaust* is a must read for middle school students. It is a touching and poignant reminder of a time in our history that had such profound effect on millions of families. Harris' recollection of his childhood journey from Poland to America is beautifully written and left me deeply moved and emotionalled drained. What a courageous man!"—**Dr. Ron Perlman**, President Illinois Resource Center.

"As World War II drew to an end, Dede Keren and I were just learning to read at the Peterson School in Chicago. Little did I dream that my beloved cousin would grow up to marry a man whose own childhood had been marked by the horrors of that war. Now Sam Harris has written the story of his survival for readers not much older than Dede and I were in those Chicago years. So Sam's book completes a circle filled with love and pain, triumph, memories, and lessons for the future."—**Susan Stamberg**, National Public Radio.

Dedication

To my parents, brothers, sisters, uncles, aunts, cousins, friends and all the six million Jews who were slaughtered in the Holocaust.

To my sisters, Rosa and Sara, without whom I would surely not have survived.

To my wife, Dede, who has brought all good blessings to me in the last thirty-eight years.

To my children, Julie and David; my son-in-law Jeff; and my grand-children, Jeremy and Jessica, for whom I am inspired to survive.

To my adoptive parents, Dr. Ellis and Harriet Harris, who provided me with a wonderful life as an American boy.

To my adoptive sister, Sue, who immediately accepted me as her big brother and who shared me with her parents when they became my parents too.

To Dede's sister and her husband, Carole and Cal Kanter, along with the other members of Dede's family who also immediately embraced me.

To my good friend, Ernest Michel, who has become my Holocaust mentor and who said to me frequently, "Sam, you owe it to share." It was destined that we met.

To my friend and confidant, Dr. Richard Kaufman, who understands and encourages me in my endeavors and who is always there for me when I need him.

Acknowledgments

I am grateful to my loving wife, Dede, who encouraged me to write and publish this book, and spent many hours proofreading and editing *Sammy.*

Comment by Samuel R. Harris

This is the true story of my childhood and the experiences I survived. When I, as a Holocaust survivor, tell of what happened, the brutality is always obvious. It is true that the most horrendous and cruel crimes were perpetrated on the Jewish people and others during the war, but I want to remind everyone that not all Germans or Polish or Ukranians were bad people. There are, and always have been, many people in every nation who are good. We should always strive to find the good in everyone, to find ways to love and not to hate. That is the message of my story.

About the Co-Author

Cheryl Gorder has been writing books since 1985. She is the author of the homeschooling bestsellers *Home Schools: An Alternative* and *Home Education Resource Guide*, both of which are currently in their fourth editions. These books have been on the Small Press Bestseller list for ten consecutive years.

Her book, *Homeless: Without Addresses in America* won the prestigious Benjamin Franklin award in 1989.

She has continued to write books on homeschooling (*Kindergarten at Home*, 1997) and social issues (*Green Earth Resource Guide*, 1991, *Multicultural Education Resource Guide,* 1996).

Working with Sam and Dede Harris on this book has been one of the most inspirational experiences of my life. I'm grateful for the opportunity not only to meet, but to work on this project with, a child survivor of the Holocaust. Sam's attitude is truly remarkable and contagious. His message will continue to be a reminder of the courageous and forgiving side of the human spirit. cg 1999

Table of Contents

7

Chapter One
Loved By All

Szlamek Rzeznik loved to run around his little village, playing with the other Jewish children—many of whom were his little cousins, and all of whom he knew very well. It was a wonderful life for a child, full of beautiful and interesting sounds, smells, sights and activities. But most of all, it was great to be loved by all.

Deblin, Poland, in the mid-1930s seemed the perfect life to Sammy, as Szlamek was affectionately called. He was surrounded by lots of family—mom, dad, brothers, sisters, cousins, aunts, uncles and grandparents. And being the youngest of his immediate family, Sammy felt special.

His dad, Shmuel Rzeznik, had been married once before, and of that marriage came three children, Chuma, Yankel and Shifra. When his wife died, he had—as was the common custom in these small Jewish towns—married his wife's younger sister, Sheva. With her, he continued his family, having Rosa, David, Sara and finally Sammy.

Sammy looked up to his dad. Shmuel was a scribe and spent many days sitting in front of the window at

9

a small desk with his books and writing instruments, carefully and painstakingly writing the Torah.* With a quill that he would dip in a black inkwell, he wrote word for word the five books of Moses.

Many books were piled on the desk, and the colors of the book bindings fascinated Sammy. Shmuel was a respected individual in the community, a teacher and a leader. But to Sammy, he was a beloved and pious father, and mostly Sammy felt very good about him.

On the Sabbath, Shmuel walked down the street in his long robes, with his hands tucked behind him and his long black beard hanging proudly. Little Sammy followed, imitating the manner and gait of his father's walk, and sometimes he even imagined himself with a long beard like his father. It was so good to be with him.

Sammy's mother, Sheva, was a beautiful woman who often played with him. No matter how much work she had, she found the time to make him feel special and show him how much she loved him.

Sheva took care of Sammy's eyes when he had polio carititis. He was almost completely blind, and often his mom took him to a dark closet where she put special eyedrops into his eyes. Eventually, his eyes healed although his vision was never fully restored, and the scars remained on the pupils of his eyes.

At this time, the older children were not living with Sammy and his parents. They were mostly married and were starting families of their own. Rosa was not yet married, as she was only seventeen, so she was often

*See Glossary in the Appendix of this book.

10

home, although she had a job in nearby Warsaw. Rosa was a beauty with long black hair and a very good dancer. She was a very likeable and uninhibited person who had a special presence about her.

Older brother David was also very special to Sammy. He was about four years older than Sammy and taught him a lot of things.

Whenever I tie my shoelaces, I think of my older brother, David, who taught me how to tie them when I was very young. I still tie my laces in that special way, under and across so that the laces look parallel to each other on the shoe.

Sabina's parents had a farm in Cholna, not far from Deblin, where the family went by horse and buggy on Friday nights, the Sabbath. Many of Sammy's aunts and uncles would be there, and he looked forward to seeing his cousins. Sammy and his sister Sara, who is one and one half years older, ran around the farm with their cousins, chasing chickens and hiding in haylofts in the barn. If the weather was nice, they stayed outside until well past dark, playing hide-and-seek games.

They eventually ended up in the hay telling scary stories, and Sara would have to hold Sammy. Usually, though, all the cousins started a tickling match, laughing and screaming with delight.

Grandma called out to the children when the challah bread was ready to come out of the oven. The aroma of the fresh bread filled the house. They watched her bend over the hot stove, her white babushka over her head, as she stuck in a large wooden spatula and pulled out the yummy treat. The children argued over who would receive the best piece. Sara liked the hard ends that went crunch, and Sammy liked that too, so they each tried to be the one to grab the first piece that Grandma cut.

Sammy's favorite place to sleep was in his grand-parents' barn when it was raining. He buried himself in the straw. The smells were sometimes so fresh, and yet other times so pungent, it seemed that his senses would overwhelm him.

There were lots of Jewish traditions for Sammy to learn, and even at four years old, he knew a lot about them. He had already learned to read, and when he was sitting at cheder with his book, he was surprised and happy to have candy dropped on his book. He thought that was fun, and didn't yet recognize that it was a Jewish tradition to keep learning sweet!

Passover stuck out in Sammy's mind: the learning of the ever-important Four Questions and reciting them, Grandfather leaning back on a pillow like a king, the opening of the door for Elijah to come, the eating and eating of matzah and drinking of wine until everyone was full. It was a long time for midnight to come for a four-year-old.

Home was comfortable to Sammy. Not fancy, but warm enough with the wood stove at one end of the two room house and the wood-burning oven for cooking at the other end. Sometimes the wood stove heated up so much it turned red all around and smoke filled the room.

Modern plumbing was not yet available to anyone in Deblin, and outhouses were common. Sammy didn't mind, though, except when it was really cold in the middle of the winter. Then he stayed snug in his nice warm bed covered up with a feather-filled quilt. He was glad there was a pot in the middle of the room for times like that when it was too difficult to go outside.

Kids had lots to do in Deblin to keep themselves entertained. One of the favorite pastimes was to swim in the overflowing Vistula River that ran near the town. Little Sammy was already a swimmer at the age of four, although he had once cut his bare foot on a piece of glass in the river. He learned to be more careful after that, because the wound hurt more than he cared to admit to his friends.

Everyone Sammy knew was Jewish, and as far as he knew, they were all pretty happy too. It was a peaceful life, full of love.

It was that love that carried me through my life.

Chapter Two
The Jewish Ghetto

"Run! Run! Get down!" Sara yelled at Sammy. He was watching the airplanes above, far too fascinated to realize that he was in danger.

Sara pushed him to safety. Sammy didn't realize it at the time, but this was to be the first of many times one of his sisters would keep him alive. And he was far too young to understand that on that day in September 1939 his life and the lives of all Jewish people in Poland were to change forever.

Deblin had an airport, and the Germans were attacking the field. It was the first that this Jewish community had directly seen of World War II, but it was not the last. Not at all.

Later that month, Sammy was playing at a neighbor's home when they heard loud noises outside. The noises grew louder and louder, and the house began to shake. The curtains in the house were drawn, so the family peeked outside to see what was going on. Tanks, motorcycles, machine guns and soldiers in steel helmets carrying guns with bayonets were going past the home, stirring up dust.

The Germans took over Deblin. They went through the town, marching and singing. Then suddenly, they dispersed and started running all over, hurting the Jews, kicking them with their hard boots and hitting them with the butts of their guns. Sammy saw people being beaten on the head and blood coming out.

It was the first time I really felt danger.

The Germans imposed curfews. The Jews were expected to remain inside with their doors and windows closed and curtains drawn. The houses were to be kept dark and quiet and nobody was to leave. Sammy's family had no electricity, only a little gas lamp. The home was dark and they tried to keep very quiet.

Sometimes they could hear noises outside, which might be a drunken German beating on doors and yelling. Frequently they heard a shot in the air. The old, the infirm and the mentally ill were taken outside of town and gassed or murdered.

The town became a ghetto right away. The Jews were forced to build a wall of barbed wire around the ghetto and pay for it, and all Jews were to live inside the ghetto.

Ghetto conditions were appalling. There was terrible overcrowding, minimum rations, and almost no contact with the outside world. Basic amenities, such as medical provisions, were not available.

Under the ration scales imposed by the Germans, Germans were entitled to 2,310 calories a day, foreigners to 1,790 calories, Poles to 934 calories and Jews to a mere 183 calories. Yet Jews had to pay twice as much as Poles, and nearly 20 times as much as Germans for each calorie. A Jew was allowed a mere three ounces of bread a day.

All comings and goings from the area were strictly monitored. People in the ghetto had to wear a star on their clothing to identify themselves as Jews. Sammy's mom made the stars and sewed them on. Hunger and sickness pervaded the community. It was very hard to obtain food. The Jewish people, in order to survive, had to smuggle food from the outside. Rosa and David became very good at this.

Rosa had returned from Warsaw, and she immediately became a leader within the family. She was smart and could speak Polish fluently, so she could leave the ghetto and people didn't know she was Jewish. Everybody liked her energy, her vibrance.

Even in time of danger, Rosa had a special way of managing to get through it. One time, she came home crying and shaking. She had been stopped by the Germans outside the ghetto and was recognized as a Jew, although she was not wearing the yellow star. That usually meant instant death, but Rosa had talked her way out of it.

When the German soldiers started gathering Jews to go to work in the slave camps, Rosa went. She worked at the nearby airfield. By doing so, she managed to get a little bit of food to share with the family. However, it was never enough and hunger pervaded. Sammy felt the hunger pains very sharply.

I shall never forget one time when my brother, David, had a little piece of stale bread. He extended his hand with the bread grasped in it to offer me a bite. I pushed my head forward to take a bigger bite than he intended. The whole piece ended in my mouth, including his finger, and I bit hard. Implanted clearly in my mind is a little red pearl of blood on his forefinger. I feel badly today just thinking about it.

Sammy was looked after by his family. Being so young, he could survive only if others shared, which they all did. But he helped as much as he could. At night they would sneak out of the ghetto and go into the countryside, hoping to find some food. The farmers had potato cellars, which were guarded by the Germans. The Jews went to the cellars to steal potatoes. If they failed, they starved. If they were caught, they were shot.

Sammy helped on these potato raids, which occurred in the darkness of night. Being small, sometimes he could squeeze into places bigger people could not. One time, he fell into a hole. The hole was all that was left of an old outhouse, but it had not been covered, so Sammy found himself covered with human waste and mud. It was a humiliating and smelly experience.

The German soldiers pretty much had their way in town. They took what they wanted, including women, as they marched through the ghetto knocking on doors.

Sammy didn't understand what they wanted, but some of the older children in the ghetto followed the soldiers and pointed and whispered.

If the German soldiers wanted food, they took it. If they didn't like someone, they either beat them or shot them. They cut off the long beards of the Jewish men. They seemed to take great pride in demoralizing people, especially those who had been pillars of the Jewish community, like Shmuel Rzeznik.

One day a soldier came to the Rzeznik home asking for some hot tea. Shmuel gave it to him, and the soldier immediately threw the tea in Shmuel's face.

It was a distinct memory. They were after him quite a bit. Four Germans took my religious and bearded father to the woods, broke off branches from trees and began beating him until he was on the ground. They continued until he could hardly move. My brother, David, was watching and crying helplessly from behind some trees. After the Germans left, he led my father home. That is when I saw my brother crying so hard. I also saw the raw wounds on my father's back as he lay on the bed, face down, in agony.

Chapter Three
Round-Up of the Deblin Jews

There was noise and commotion outside. The Germans were going to Jewish homes, rounding up the people and pulling them outside. People were yelling and screaming, and Germans were shouting at them and threatening them.

Now, in 1942, the German soldiers were busy rounding up the Deblin Jews, as they had done in so many Polish cities before this. The unfortunates who were pulled into the lines were herded into cattle cars on the train and moved to Treblinka, Auschwitz or to be gassed and burned.

In Deblin, Sammy heard all of the screaming as he and his family were pulled into one of the many deep lines of people. He was frightened. Now seven years old, he didn't completely understand what was going on, but he had a pretty strong idea that it was not good.

To small Sammy, the long thick lines of adults were like a forest of legs. All he saw were legs, unless he moved his head up. Then he could see the sky.

The sky was dark, thick, misty and very low.

19

I could almost touch it as I felt my face moistened by the very fine drizzle. It was as if the skies were crying on us.

Sammy was squashed by the mass of humanity. He could not move his arms because he was packed in the middle of the herd of Jews that were being sent on a train ride. His face had to point upward so that he could breathe.

As I stared into that sky, I remember thinking and praying. Something told me that I would live and be okay. This is the only time I really prayed so deeply and felt some communication and assurance. It was as though an angel was reassuring me.

"Go! Run! Over there to Sara!" Sammy's dad pushed him out of the line toward his sister Sara, who was already hiding behind some bricks. Sara held his hand tightly. They were both so terrified that they kept very, very quiet.

The lines of people started moving, slowly because there were so many of them. Still the German soldiers yelled at them and told them to move faster, which was impossible because of the sheer numbers of them. Soldiers beat on people as they passed by, and the Jews could do little but just keep moving in the direction of the train. People were crying, some loudly and others softly, as they marched onward.

They were marched to the cattle cars that took them directly to the gas chambers. In my mind, they are still marching. On these lines were my father, two sisters, a brother, many cousins, friends and neighbors. As the moving lines got smaller and the crying voices got softer, I looked into the sky and knew I would be all right.

All of the relatives were taken away to be gassed. Sammy never had a chance to say good-bye, and he never saw them again. He sensed that something terrible was going to happen to them.

Rosa devoted her life to taking care of Sammy and Sara. Without her, there was no prayer of either one of them surviving. They had to hide now. They survived on crumbs and scraps that Rosa managed to bring to them, but hunger was a constant problem.

Hunger was a problem to all of the remaining Jews in Deblin as well. Often on the streets there would be signs of starvation, such as a person lying on the street swollen and bloated from lack of food. Sammy sometimes was so hungry he wished he didn't have to live any more. But he kept on going. The angel had told him he would live.

The second time the soldiers went about gathering the Jews, they started shooting. Hundreds of people were shot and left to lie in the streets. Rosa, Sara and Sammy didn't see the shooting start, but they heard it, so they started running. They ran and ran and ran. Sammy felt somehow empowered, as if he could run faster and jump higher than ever before. Somehow his angel, despite Sammy's hunger and loss of strength, had given him tremendous energy. He never looked back at whoever was shooting behind him, and he was never sure if he was being directly shot at or not.

The children found an outhouse on a Polish farm where they hid and listened to the noises, huddling together in fear. Soon the door was yanked open. It was the Polish farmer. He chased them out of the outhouse and off his property. They ran again.

The shooting was coming closer and closer. Sammy could see the helmets of the German soldiers in the distance. Ahead of them was another farmhouse. Rosa noticed a board missing on the top of the barn and told Sara to climb up there. Sammy was also pushed up. Then Rosa came through the small opening.

They rested and hid in the straw, pulling the hay over them, covering their whole bodies, faces and heads so that they could not be seen. They could still hear shooting in the background.

"Juden Raus, Jews get out!" the German soldiers shouted outside the barn. Sammy's fear was beyond description. The soldiers continued to yell as they ran through the countryside and searched for Jews. The shooting went on until dark.

Eventually, Rosa, Sara and Sammy climbed out of the straw and went back to their home. It was dark, but Sammy could make out piles in the street, which he assumed were garbage. Rosa sent him to bed.

Early the next morning I got up and went outside. Then I saw one of the most horrible sights I had ever seen. No, that was not garbage piled outside. Those were dead people, stacked one on top of the other. Those were our neighbors.

They walked around to see who all was lying in the pile. Other people also gathered around, trying to identify which of their friends had died during the previous day's shooting.

I noticed something stirring in the pile among the dead. There was movement on the bottom. Several of the grownups untangled the bodies. It was a small child. Pulled out from under the mass of human flesh, this child began to cry.

In the midst of all of this horror, the Polish towns-people began going around and removing items from the dead people, such as watches or anything of value. They didn't seem at all concerned or sad about the tragedy.

That really bothered me as a kid. There was no crying, and it left a pointed impression. It made me angry at the Polish people at the time, because I didn't know them as individuals, but rather as a callous people who didn't seem bothered by what had happened to the Jews.

Survival was becoming harder and harder for the remaining Deblin Jews. Yet somehow, Rosa kept her group together and alive.

Chapter Four
Deblin Concentration Camp

Although most of the Jews in Deblin had been rounded up and transported to the gas chambers, the Germans did keep a select few of the Jews to work. Rosa, being so smart, strong and alert, was kept working. David had gone off with another family to have a better chance, since Rosa already had the responsibility of keeping Sara and Sammy alive. The whole town was supposed to be free of Jews now, as two transports had gone away with them.

The few that remained, including Rosa, were kept in a concentration camp that had been erected. It was a big thing to be in that concentration camp. If you weren't working there, you would be shot.

Rosa was allowed to go there and live. At first, Sara and Sammy could not get in the camp, so Rosa gave them to a Polish friend to take care of them temporarily. The friend's husband became drunk that night, and heard on the radio that any Pole found hiding a Jew would also be shot. He told his wife that he was going to turn the children in.

Knowing that the children could not stay with her

any more, Rosa's friend sent Sammy to one family and Sara to another.

It was becoming even more dangerous now. Any Jew found outside the concentration camp was shot immediately. Some people managed to escape to the woods, but most of them were hunted down by German armed units and massacred. Others died of starvation, cold and disease. A few hundred who survived the repeated searches and the ravages of winter were called partisans, and remained hidden in the forest.

Partisans faced full-scale German military campaigns, local hostility and betrayal by Poles. They had no medical help, little food, brackish water, and extremes in climate, including sub-zero winter weather. Few survived. Yet the spirit of resistance was strong.

While Sammy waited for Rosa, he was forced to live in a potato cellar with about twenty other Jews.

I remember climbing down a ladder into a very dark, cold room. The floor was wet and muddy. The ceiling seemed very high up. At the top of the ceiling was a small round glass covering through which some sunlight shined. School children banged on that glass and yelled in Polish, "Dirty Jews!" I was scared. Soon the sun set, and there was no light shining through that glass opening into that cold cellar. I started to shiver. Somehow, I was able to locate a broken wooden chair with half of its seat gone. I sat on that chair all night with very little sleep. No one spoke. I wished I had a blanket, or food, or most of all, someone to comfort me. I was alone without my sisters or parents.

After about a day, Sammy was hoisted out of the cellar and told that Rosa had made arrangements for him to sneak into the concentration camp. When he arrived there, Sara was already waiting for him. She lifted the barbed wire for him to get in. Walking by a fenced-in area, he heard German shepherd dogs barking nearby. He shivered, as much from fright as from the cold.

Concentration camp became a haven, my ticket to safety. Otherwise I would have gone straight to the gas chambers or been shot on sight. I would have joined the 1,500,000 Jewish children that were slaughtered.

The concentration camp contained barracks for the Jews, some for women and others for men. Inside the barracks were wooden bunks several rows high with straw and burlap bags for sleeping. Since Sammy was too young to work, he needed to keep clear of the guards, and so most of his time was spent in the darkness. The Germans were always around, pacing outside to make sure no one could sneak away.

The scanty meals consisted of very thin soup which was merely boiled water with a very little horse meat, and served in an old rusty can that one carried all the time. A lucky person might get a small piece of meat. Rosa somehow was able to work something out to get a little food to share with Sara and Sammy.

Shootings and beatings by guards were common. They didn't need much of an excuse to be brutal to the Jews. Sometimes the Jews would try to escape, but they were usually caught. If they made it to the woods, they would join the partisans who were trying to survive there. But usually they didn't make it. The Germans brought them back and hanged them between the barracks and the outhouses for several days as a reminder of what happened to escapees. Their bodies hung between the barracks.

Sammy never witnessed an actual hanging of an escapee, but he did see the bodies hanging between the barracks and the outhouses. If he left his hiding place, he was faced with this kind of scene. So, often, he preferred not to go to the outhouse, especially at night, as it was far too frightening to him. Instead, bedwetting became a problem for him, but this was far more bearable than walking past the hanging dead people.

My first memory of this problem is of someone yelling in the darkness from a bed bunker below me, "It's dripping! Stop that!" The disturbance awakened about two hundred people. The lights went on in the barracks of the concentration camp.

28

The bedwetting caused Sammy's burlap sack to be continually wet all day from the night before. He would purposely lie on the wet parts of the sack, hoping that his body would dry the area. He never achieved that. Instead, the straw began to stink, and the sack became rotten and a big hole appeared in the middle.

Fungus grew around the hole and caused it to become fuzzy and greenish. Soon there were many flies and lice in my bed and in my clothing. But what hurt the most were the gashes on my hips and sides from the infection that came from lying on the rotten burlap sack. Conditions were bad enough for people in the concentration camp. They didn't need a kid causing all that trouble, a kid who was trying to hide there unnoticed by the Germans. I do not remember the physical pain, but the fears and embarrassment I felt then were the worst of my life.

Sammy chose wetting the bed and getting infected as the better alternative to having to go past those dead people hanging and swaying back and forth on the ropes outside the barracks. This choice caused him great pain, but we can understand why he made it.

Near the concentration camp was a rail line where trains traveled past with loads of people. Sammy witnessed people sticking their hands out of the cattle cars, screaming and yelling and crying. He knew that they were on their way to something terrible, and it was a horrible sight for him to see.

In the concentration camps, each person did his best to do what he could to survive. But Rosa had two extra mouths to feed. To earn extra bread to feed Sammy and Sara, Rosa took on additional work washing underwear which was no easy task because people had no toilet paper. She frequently threw up.

Occasionally there was even a joyful event. Walter, a wonderful Viennese Jew, was in charge of the disinfection showers. Rosa worked in the same location washing underwear. While in the Deblin Concentration Camp they fell in love and married. Because they were not in a regular setting, they did the best they could. They could not live together because men and women had to live in separate barracks.

Now Sammy had a brother-in-law, a new role model, and one more person who cared about his survival. Walter loved Rosa very much and was committed to helping her care for her two siblings. Again, luck was helping Sammy survive.

Chapter Five
Simchas Torah

In the Deblin concentration camp in the spring of 1944, nine-year-old Sammy sensed that something different was happening. He heard people talking with excitement and he could hear vibrations. The war was closing in on Deblin.

The Germans decided to move the Jewish workers from the Deblin camp to Czestochowa, a camp farther away. In that camp the Jews were forced to make bullets for the war.

There were two transports from Deblin to Czestochowa at this time. Most of the Jews were taken in the first transport, about a thousand in all, including most of the twenty children who were in the Deblin camp. All but five children were taken in the first train. The Jews were put on a cattle car and taken away. The people who were leaving were crying and didn't want to go. They knew that the Deblin camp was as good a place as you could be if you were a Jew in Poland, and everyone knew where all of those cattle cars that kept passing by were going.

There was a little Yiddish song about the journey:

Treblinka Dort
Far yedn Yid ayn bitern ort
Ver geyt shoyn hin
Er komt nit rang

Unsere yidn in
Yene zayt yam
Zi kenen night filn
Unsere biter schmerts

Translation:

Treblinka over there for every Jew a bitter place
Whoever goes in doesn't come out.

Our Jews on the other side of the ocean
They cannot feel our terrible pain.

No one really knew if the first transport was taking people to Treblinka or to Czestochowa. Even young Sammy realized that he and his sisters were fortunate not to have to go on that first transport. Because his new brother-in-law, Walter, was in charge of the bathhouse, he was able to convince the Nazis to keep Rosa and the children in the Camp. Also, he spoke German, and the Germans needed him.

The remaining Jewish laborers, including Walter, Rosa, Sammy and Sara, went on a second train to Czestochowa as the Russians were approaching. They were locked into the cattle cars.

> *Most of the cars were completely enclosed*
> *with barbed wires in the little windows near*
> *the top of the cars. I was in an open car*
> *with no top. There were a lot of people in*
> *there with little room to move around. As*
> *we approached the railroad crossing, I*
> *could hear bells starting softly and getting*
> *louder as we got closer to the crossing. Then*
> *quickly the bells would fade away.*

Sammy was aware of the constant rhythm of the train, *ta tum ta tum ta tum ta tum*, as it hit each rail. He could hear the puffing and chugging of the engine. The outside seemed so silent, and everyone was so very cold and hungry.

When they would come close to the crossroads, Sammy heard the children yelling, playing, having fun and the dogs barking. How he wished that he could be out there! Anywhere but here! He wished he were a dog or anything, but not on a train feeling hungry and scared. He didn't want to be one of those people being carried away on the cattle trains with their hands hanging out and crying and shouting. He knew that wherever he was going, it probably was not good.

> *We were riding at night. When I looked up*
> *at the stars, I do not remember seeing the*
> *moon. Sometime early in the morning, the*

*train stopped. We were told to be very quiet.
When one man stepped on another man's
shoulder to look over the side of the car,
we heard a shot fired by a German guard.
The man was not hit, but he said there was
nothing but woods out there. It was quiet
and peaceful, almost ominous. After awhile
the train started to move and the soot and
sparks of the engine sprayed on us again.
Our next and last stop was not so quiet.
I could hear voices speaking and yelling
in German. Then the heavy doors of those
freight cars were opened.*

Sammy saw people being pushed down a steep
wooden ramp from the car, and hit and pushed by the
Germans who carried bayonetted guns and whips. Some
of them had barking dogs held on leashes.

When the first transport came into Czestochowa
camp, a man appeared. It was his job to separate the
people, children to the left and others to the right. The
children were loaded onto a truck and taken to the woods
where they were shot by the German soldiers.

On the second transport from Deblin, Sammy got
out of the cattle car, and he was forced to go to the left
even though he had stood on the tips of his toes. Knowing
he could be taken away if he was too small, Rosa and
Walter told him to stand on his tiptoes. That way he
would look big enough to be a worker. Sammy strained
and strained and tried to look as tall as possible, but the

German pulled him away from his sisters and forced him to go to the left along with four other children. Rosa and Sara could only watch and cry.

> *This was one of the most frightening experi-*
> *ences of my life. People were pushed into*
> *separate lines, men in one line, women*
> *in another, and children in a third line.*
> *There were only five children and I was*
> *one of them. The children's relatives were*
> *screaming and crying but they were beaten*
> *away. I was kicked in the chest by a German.*
> *I still remember that shiny boot that was*
> *tailored around his leg. I don't remember*
> *the pain, just the boot.*

The children were placed in a room just outside the barbed wire gates leading into the main camp. Sammy could see the gates through a window in that room. The adults were leaning on the gates, crying, yelling and glaring in the direction of the children's window about a hundred yards away, hoping to see the five children who were taken from them. They knew that the children would soon be taken by truck to the woods and be shot.

Sammy was entirely aware of the seriousness of his situation and distraught at being separated from his sisters. Yet he continued to feel that somehow he would be all right.

> *In my mind, I did not think of death. I still*

35

had faith in my survival with thoughts of crossing the nearby river I saw through the window, of jumping from the trucks and just running. I gave the Ukranian soldier guarding us a little note to give to my sisters when they were crying by the barbed wire gate. The note, written in Yiddish, said not to worry about me. I would be all right. My sisters still talk about this note.

The children stayed in that room for several days. Crying people continued to flock to the gate, waiting, waving and praying for their release.

One evening, there was a commotion outside. A Jew was arguing in German with an SS officer.

"The papers say Ruthie is to be allowed to stay with me!" shouted the Jew, who happened to be a man of some importance to the Germans. Because of his position, he had been given papers before leaving Deblin that said his daughter would be allowed to stay with him in Czestochowa.

"What is said in Deblin does not matter here!" shouted back the SS officer.

"Then look at the signature and tell me you don't care about that signature!" The Jew thrust the papers at the officer.

The German looked at the papers and then sulkingly shook his head. "OK, she can go with you. But the others stay!"

"ALL THE CHILDREN OR NONE!" shouted the

36

Jew, hoping to allow all the children to be spared. Everyone held their breath, knowing that this man was risking his own daughter's life to save the other children.

"ALL OR NONE!" he shouted again.

This time the German just shrugged his shoulders and walked away. Then with a motion of his hand, he nodded to a guard to let the children out.

The children were taken out of the room and led toward the main concentration camp. The people, many of whom had lost their own children, were overjoyed at seeing these little people. Many were crying and praying out loud.

As Sammy passed the barbed wire gates into the camp, he was lifted up, kissed and hugged, and passed overhead from hand to hand. These men and women, who hadn't seen a Jewish child in years, reverently passed Sammy from one person to another, in the manner that the Torah is handed from person to person on the festival of Simchas Torah.

> *The Torah must feel the same as I did when passed from hand to hand. I can still see their faces, feel their love. I have always felt the responsibility, weight and burden of fulfilling their hope. Every year at the celebration of Simchas Torah, I think of the gift of life given to me in the Czestochowa concentration camp.*

Deblin Ghetto

Czestochowa Concentration Camp

Partial Map of Poland

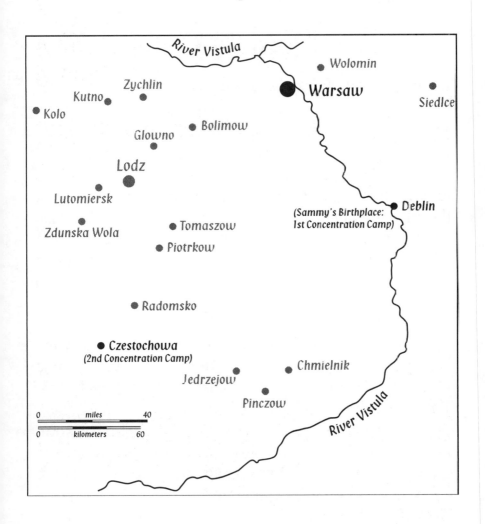

Chapter Six
Czestochowa
Concentration Camp

No one was happier than Sammy when he was reunited with his sisters. They were together again. But the fact remained they were living in a concentration camp where children were not welcome. The children who had managed to enter the camp were still at risk of being shot any time a German felt like it, so they had to hide all the time. They could not risk being seen by any of the German guards.

Any time an SS officer or guard came near, the Jews would whistle, and the children would run and hide — either under the bunks or under the straw in the bunks. They occasionally had narrow escapes.

One time, Sara didn't hear the whistle soon enough. She dove into a bunk and just barely had time to cover herself with the burlap bag that was on top of the straw before the guard came in to inspect the barracks. He walked along the corridor, and looked in and out of the bunks. He ran his hands along the burlap on the bunks, then he left.

The most terrifying experience of the concentration camp for Sara was when he ran his hands along the burlap sack. She was hiding underneath, holding her breath and praying that he would not discover her.

The Jewish laborers at this camp made lead bullets for the war. Every morning and every night, Jews were rounded up in the camp and marched off to work shifts in the factory. Since Sammy was a child and not old enough to work in the factory, he usually had to hide in the barracks. However, one hot and humid evening, he took a chance and marched with his sisters to the factory.

We marched into a big room, lit by electricity, smelling of oil, and very noisy with the sound of machines running. I saw long belts turning wheels and milky water flowing to cool the machines. Pitiful, skinny emaciated men and women worked the machines while the guards intimidated them.

Lead coils the size of bicycle wheels were lying by the machines. They must have weighed from fifty to one hundred pounds each. The machines cut off lead chunks about one and a half inches long and filled the tips of bullets with the chunks.

I remember five or six men with unshaven faces and hollow cheeks pacing back and forth and slipping on the wet floor. These

41

men were all wearing dirty, greasy-looking striped pajama-type clothing. They were in great agony because they had to walk many hours inside the factory carrying those heavy lead coils around their necks. I remember those poor men were being punished for not being able to keep up the pace of work. They were walking, limping and struggling with those weights around their necks, not only for punishment, but also to show the other slave laborers what would happen to them if they did not work fast.

Rosa and Sara worked on the machines along with other women. Sammy watched the scene all night until he could not keep his eyes open. He saw a basket nearby and crawled into it and fell asleep.

Suddenly I felt a hard slap on my left cheek and heard someone yelling at me in German! I opened my eyes and, trembling with fear, saw an ugly German woman with long brown hair standing over me continuing to yell. Apparently she was surprised that I was only a child. Later that night, the same woman gave me half of her sandwich. I would have gladly taken a slap on the other cheek for the other half of the sandwich.

Sammy and his sisters marched back to the barracks without further incident that night.

Hunger, filth, lice, fleas and disease were constant companions to the Jews in the camps. The people turned into hungry, pale, malnourished skeletons. The toil, the beatings and the diseases were all around them.

A tall wall with German and Ukranian guards on top surrounded the barracks where the Jews lived, and the barracks surrounded the bullet factory where the Jews worked. Near the barracks was a pipe from the factory that gushed out hot steam.

Using that steam to cook potatoes was a delicacy for the Jews. All they had to do was obtain the potatoes, take an old can, fill it with water, and put potatoes into it. At night, Sammy would place the steam pipe into the can of water, holding it there until the potatoes were cooked.

Steaming them was the easy part. The major problem was where to get the potatoes. A tall barbed wire gate separated the barracks from the area where a freight car loaded with potatoes was rolled in on the tracks from time to time. Sammy became an expert little thief of potatoes, as he was small and could squeeze between the barbed wire rows if someone spread them apart for him. In the dark, he was able to get to the potato car, climb to the top and get potatoes.

His shabby old coat had a lining with a hole in the inside pocket. This was where he put the potatoes. When the coat was filled, it would scrape the ground, which made it more difficult for him to walk or run. He was such a sight that he made even the most physically and emotionally miserable Jewish prisoner laugh as he came dragging those potatoes. He stole potatoes many times that way and got by with it.

One night, he crossed between the barbed wire and looked to see where the armed guard was walking. He seemed far away. Sammy walked into the big dark warehouse to check it out for more guards.

Suddenly from nowhere a soldier yelled, grabbed me by the arm and held his revolver right in front of my eyes. I was shaking frantically, filled with fear. Looking into his eyes, I saw the most cold, reptilian look I had ever seen in a human being. I didn't know what to do. Then the soldier let go of my arm. His revolver was still pointing at my eyes. I wondered if I would die. Instead, I turned and ran as quickly as my feet would carry me. He chased me. I ran into a wide and deep ditch and had trouble climbing out at the other end. The soldier stopped in front of the ditch just as I made it over the other side. He must have decided to let the little scared fellow go. I can still see the barrel of his revolver. I shake to this day when I think of it.

Chapter Seven
Liberation

The skies were all lit up, pink and red and white.
It looked like fireworks to the slaves of the concentration camp. Because of the high walls surrounding them,
all they could see of the outside of the camp was the sky.
Now it was very colorful. But it wasn't from any cel-
ebration going on outside the concentration camp. It was
bombings from the war. And it was getting closer.

The Jews put their ears to the ground and listened.
They could feel the vibrations of exploding bombs. They
heard the blasts coming closer and closer, but they could
not see them. The only window they had to the outside
world was the sky.

*We could see the reflections of fires in the
sky as these noises and vibrations were
nearing our camp. We could hear great
blasts all around us, but could not see
because there were no windows. As the
evening progressed, I turned my head
upward and saw a myriad of lights reflected*

*from the smoke and dark sky above. We
began to dare to think of the start of a new
beginning.*

Yet even now, the Germans were determined to
keep on sending the Jews to the gas chambers. They
had people start lining up to be removed to Auschwitz.
Sammy and his family were among the first ones in this
line as it was being done alphabetically, and Rosa's new
last name was Appel.

*The guards were still pacing with guns in
their hands on top of the walls. We could
see the reflection of light from those burning
fires on their faces. They almost appeared
human. They were frightened too. The
Germans on the ground seemed confused,
hurried and disorganized. They didn't know
whether to shoot the Jews or to run.*

Suddenly, there was screaming and yelling and
the Germans abandoned their posts from the tops of the
buildings. The officers lining up Sammy and his family
decided it was time to make a hasty exit. As they left,
the Jews started to scream with pleasure. Some were
crying, and others shouting.

*The Jews inside the walls were happy, full
of smiles, kisses and hugs. Soon I could see
several Jews climbing the walls to take the*

guns from soldiers on top.

The sky was getting brighter and brighter with the light of the bombings, but to the Jews it was not frightening. Instead, it gave them great pleasure as it indicated their liberation from the Germans.

> *Our heads were always poised upwards toward the sky. The sights we saw were even more exciting than the sights at Disneyland in front of Cinderella Castle at midnight. Yes, we were free! Years later, when I saw the band playing in Fantasyland and firecrackers exploded over the Disneyland castle, I was thinking of how it was then, and I prayed, "God bless America."*

They were free!! Free at last! Free from the brutal Germans and Ukranians. Free to start a new beginning.

The Jews didn't know exactly what to do, however, with their new-found freedom. They were running all over the camp, trying to decide what to do next. One man ran into the Germans' quarters and came out with food. Everyone ate ravenously, as they were starving. Sammy was handed a round ball of butter that looked as big as a football to him. He wolfed the whole thing down. It was his first taste of real food in years. Sammy did get sick from the pound of butter, but the joy he felt was greater than the pain.

Sammy's sisters, along with Walter and some other Jews, decided to leave the camp. There were no more Germans and the gates were open. Just before dawn, they left the camp. It was misty out, and eerily silent. In the distance, they heard some noises. One Jew said, "Let's go back."

But Walter said, "No, we're better out here."

Soon they heard two people talking to each other in a foreign tongue. It was Russian. The Russians were moving in, and they waved Sammy and his family to go behind them. The Jews moved farther and farther away from the gates. They could hear shooting in the distance. Dawn was approaching. They began to see the results of last night's drama unfold in front of them — bodies of soldiers all around, some Russian, some German. Some of the Jews were kicking and spitting on the dead Nazis. The Russians, sitting on their tanks with their machine guns, kept waving them to go farther.

Sammy found the sight of the Russian machine guns and the sound of the Russian soldiers singing to be exciting, even though he was freezing cold. It was January 17, 1945, and the cold was penetrating through the rags he had bound around his feet with string. He hadn't had real shoes in years, and the cold was unbearable. Still, he and his family plodded on in their freedom.

They tried to stay with some Polish farmers, but were shooed away. Eventually, they ended up in a room with about twenty survivors.

When the Russians liberated Poland, the Jews, not knowing where to go, went to familiar territory: their homes. So Rosa, Walter, Sara and Sammy went back to Deblin. They stayed overnight, but decided it was not going to be safe there.

The Jewish people were not being greeted nicely by the Polish people. In fact, many of the Polish farmers and townspeople were threatening the Jews with axes. Some Jews were killed.

Sammy had survived a Jewish ghetto and two concentration camps, and still he found persecution in his own country. It had been many years since life had been normal, and it was going to take longer yet.

Chapter Eight
The Orphanage

Rosa, Walter, Sara and Sammy had survived. Now it was decision-time. What next? What to do? Where to go? How to survive now?

There were a lot of questions, but few answers. It was obvious it was not going to be easy for the Jews to survive, even though they had been liberated. After long deliberation, Rosa and Walter decided their best chance was to get back to Walter's hometown in Austria to find any surviving members of his family. They left Sammy and Sara in an orphanage in Lublin, Poland, telling them that they would be back to get them as soon as they could.

Once again, Sammy was separated from people he loved. Although everyone treated him kindly at the orphanage, it wasn't quite like his family life in Deblin before the war. The boys and girls were kept separate most of the time, and they all had to wear the same clothing. Of course, they all had something in common: they had no parents any more.

The children were a bedraggled sight. They had little clothing, and most had no shoes. They were a flea and lice-ridden group, with poor health rampant. Many had their heads shaved to control the bugs. Volunteers brought supplies when possible, and eventually medicine and food became available. Sammy started to eat normally. One of the things the children were required to eat was a little red pill. This was probably some sort of vitamin or medicine, but to Sammy, it was a treat. He ate as many as he could get.

The older children started going to a Polish school. Sammy began to learn more Polish. However, the children at the school would taunt him. After class, some would beat him or throw rocks at him because he was Jewish.

Sammy coped with this situation as best he could, for he always tried to look for the best solution in life. Already, at ten years old, he had developed a unique perspective. He realized that he was one of the few Jewish child survivors of the war. He felt he had a responsibility to carry on, to multiply and to be an example that Jews are good. He had seen the deaths of many Jews, of many of his friends and relatives, and he already was trying to plan ahead to do his best in life.

Weeks and months went by. Rosa had not yet returned.

One day Sammy and Sara were riding bikes. Sammy had just learned how to ride, so he was at the top of a hill. Because it was easier to ride down the hill than up, he was there with the intention of coasting and riding down that hill. A friend was holding onto the rear of Sammy's bike, ready to let him go. All of a sudden, he heard Sara squeal.

"Rosa!" she cried.

Sammy saw a figure on the road approaching where he was about to ride. Sure enough, there was Rosa, with her arms held out for her brother and sister. Sammy threw down the bike and ran to her, his eyes full of grateful tears.

"You did come back for us!" he said.

"Of course. I said I would!" said Rosa.

Once again, the family was united. This time war was not going to separate them. Rosa had earned enough money to bribe Russian soldiers to bring her where she had left her family, and to help her get the children out of Poland and into Austria. She was still very clever and energetic, and able to make things happen.

Since they had virtually no belongings, the children were very quickly loaded into the truck that was waiting.

Two Russian soldiers dressed in long, warm coats, black leather boots and hats with earmuffs waited by the truck. The soldiers opened the doors at the rear of the truck. It was completely filled from floor to ceiling with barrels of oil and gas. They asked us to climb in and move through a passage to the middle where two barrels had already been taken out. Sara and I sat in this space while the Russians refilled the passage with barrels they had removed. That little space was cold, dark and scary. It also became

SAMMY: Child Survivor of the Holocaust

Above: Orphanage in 1945.
Sara and Sam circled.

53

Orphanage photos. Above: Sam first row left. Below, Sam is third row, fifth position, and Sara is back row, fourth from right, both circled.

very bumpy as the truck began to move.
Hours passed by slowly.

They had to stop at various checkpoints along the way because they were traveling from Poland through Czechoslovakia to Austria. At these checkpoints, the truck was opened and the cargo inspected. At those times, Sammy and his sisters were frightened.

At night, the truck came to a halt at a house on a small farm. What a pleasure it was to warm up and eat. When it was time to sleep, I shared a bed with a Russian soldier, Boris, who showed me his revolver before he placed it under the pillow and we fell asleep.

They continued the next day until they made it to Vienna. Boris taught Sammy to play chess, but was upset that Sammy learned so quickly that he won the second game they played.

A second liberation had been gained, this time a liberation from Poland to Vienna.

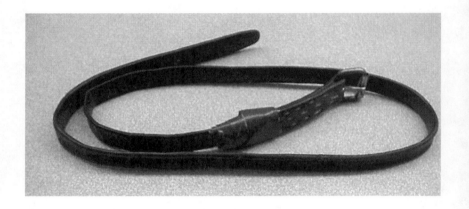

Sammy's belt.

Chapter Nine
If Only My Belt Could Speak

The only item that Sammy had after surviving the Jewish ghetto, the two concentration camps, and liberation was a skinny belt that he found in a closet in the Deblin concentration camp. This item became very special to him and he has it to this day. He says:

I have a darkish brown belt that is skinny, about a quarter of an inch wide. It is cracked from age and dryness and would probably break in two if worn. As a matter of fact, the buckle and leather attached to it are already broken off from the rest of the belt. I tape them together just so it can be one belt again.

I asked myself, "Why is this belt made of durable leather broken?" I am sad that it has not lasted. It is my friend. It is the only physical item that I have left from childhood in camps . . . in Nazi concentration camps.

SAMMY: Child Survivor of the Holocaust

Come look at this belt. It speaks! It speaks of the growling pain of hunger in a child's thin tummy. It speaks of sights it has seen and feelings it has felt on others. Oh, little belt, keep talking. Thank you for being with me and for holding my shabby, torn pants as I made it through those dark days.

I am very sorry that you cracked apart. Even if you had stayed together, you would not now fit around my big belly. However, I will keep you and remember you forever.

Chapter Ten
The Beautiful Lady of Liberty

Life in Vienna was better than what Sammy had known in many years. Walter and Rosa took good care of him and Sara. He no longer experienced the hunger and pain which had been unwelcome guests in his life for so long.

He also attended regular school in Vienna and was learning German. He had just started learning Polish in the Deblin school, and now he was learning German. Placed in the third garde, Sammy did well in his studies, both religious and secular. But even in Vienna, the school children would taunt him because he was Jewish. They threatened him all of the time, and it became uncomfortable having to face them every day. One day the biggest kid in the class waited for him after school. By now, Sammy was no longer a skinny little kid, and he had some size. So he picked up this kid, swung him around, lowered him on his knee and then spanked him. From then on, the other kids treated him more like a hero than a victim.

The family learned about the fate of their brother

David. He had been sent to a different camp than they had, and they had lost track of him. However, they learned through the grapevine that he had been killed just two weeks before the end of the war while sneaking out of the camp to get a beet from a field.

Rosa was a very caring sister, and she was concerned about the future of Sara and Sammy in Vienna. Walter and Rosa were aware that Vienna might not be the best place for the children to live their lives. They might have a better chance of a good life if they went elsewhere. Europe after the war was still unkind to the Jews. Sending the children to be adopted in either Israel or the United States would give them a chance to grow up where their religion would not be a hindrance. It was a tremendous sacrifice for Walter and Rosa to give up the children they loved, but they, too, were still very much struggling to survive after the brutal war. Rosa gave birth to a little boy and named him Herman after Walter's father.

Sammy was twelve when Rosa and Walter decided to send him and Sara to the United States to be adopted. Rosa had one more thing that she wanted to happen before Sammy left. They all went to a synagogue where a rabbi was waiting. He said some prayers, and conducted a little service. It was not a formal bar mitzvah, the Jewish coming-of-age tradition for young men, but it was something that Rosa felt would keep Sammy following

EMBARKATION CARD
Einschiffungskarte

ERNIE PYLE

S/S _____

Sailing-Date: **11. Sep. 1947**

Accommodation *C 20 - 91*
Schiffsplatz

Mr.
~~Mrs.~~
~~Miss~~
RZEZNIK, Samuel

Nr. 21 A 850

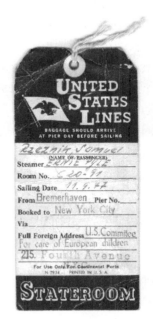

Above: Embarcation card.
Right: Ticket to the ship, Ernie Pyle.

his Jewish tradition throughout his life.

Once again, Sammy's life was changed forever, and he was forced to leave people he loved. This time, however, it was to move forward to a better life. Life was starting to turn in a different direction. This journey was full of anticipation.

The children packed their few belongings and went by train to Bremerhafen, Germany. They stopped at cities along the way to pick up other Jewish children. They stopped and toured the crematorium at Dachau. This left a strong impression on Sammy, as he had never before seen the inside of the final stop of many of the Jewish people he had loved. He saw the bones piled up, the ovens and the ashes. The reality of what happened to his family was overwhelming. More than ever, he was determined to make something of his life to make up for those who had not survived.

The children boarded a ship called the Ernie Pyle, an old military ship named after an American news reporter who had died in the war. There were other children on this ship, but Sammy didn't get to know them well. It was a very rocky trip, and the children were often sick. One time Sammy was on deck when it was rough passage, and he nearly was washed overboard. After that, he was careful to stay near a railing for safety. New York City was their destination, and, as they drew near, the excitement increased.

I remember being on the ship Ernie Pyle, leaning over the railing and watching

New York come closer to me. I was staring silently. All kinds of thoughts went through my twelve-year-old mind. Where will I go? How do I learn to speak English? With whom will I stay? What about the customs of this land?

"There she is!"

"Where? I don't see her. Oh, yes! Now I do!"

For the first time, through the haze on the water and through my thick eyeglasses, I saw a figure, the most beautiful figure I had ever seen.

I was very excited. It was the figure that every immigrant crossing the Atlantic and sailing towards New York looks for and finds. The figure that greets you so warmly, like a mother after you have been lost.

Even if you have never seen her, you know that I am speaking of the Statue of Liberty. Seeing her for the first time as a newcomer is a special feeling. That glory is difficult for me to explain to anyone other than an immigrant such as myself. She was the most beautiful and magnificent sight I had ever seen.

My mind was full of dreams—dreams of my future.

Chapter Eleven
I Am Home

There were only three English words that Sammy understood when he landed in New York City: yes, no, and Coca-Cola. Sammy and Sara had been brought over by the U.S. Committee for Care of European Children. Members of the committee led them to a temporary holding home after which the counselors showed them the city via the New York City train system.

They took the children to the top of the Empire State Building. Sammy thought it was awesome. They were shown other places of interest, and during the trip they changed trains. With all of the crowds pushing, Sammy was cut off from his group. He looked about frantically, but could not see anyone he recognized.

The train took off, and he was alone on the platform. Alone. Could not speak English. New York City. It was not fun. What could he do? He waited for the next train and got off at the next station.

No one was waiting for me. I did this for several stops and never found a soul that

*was familiar. I walked down the elevated
train station and began to look for a familiar
surrounding. I saw nothing. It was getting
dark. I was becoming more frantic.*

Sammy stopped an elderly lady and asked her in
German if she spoke German. She shrugged her shoulders. He tried again with several other people. Nothing
helped. He remembered that the street he had been staying on was perpendicular to the elevated train and he
saw busses that seemed to go underneath the elevated
train. He got into one bus and stood by the window and
watched as each street passed by.

*I had no identification with me. I had no
address with me of where we lived. My mind
was blank. It was getting dark and I was
getting more scared each moment as the
neon lights began to shine on the streets.*

Sammy got off the bus and began to walk down
the street. After about an hour, suddenly he saw something familiar. He had found the place. What a miracle!
An angel must have led him back, as he did not have
a clue where to go.

The worst part was that no one had even missed
him.

There was a family in New York that Sammy really
wanted to meet. Their name was Lester, and they had
been sending "care packages" to him in Vienna when

he lived with Rosa. Many Americans had been sending such packages, having received the address of a European child from an organization. The Lesters had wanted to help an orphan. Sammy had been the recipient of these kind packages containing clothing and food and long, loving letters that were very comforting. Those packages, and especially the letters, had made Sammy feel very important and special.

The Lester family came for Sammy and took him for a ride. Mr. and Mrs. Lester and their son, Oliver, who was much older than I, were eager to see in person the lad to whom they had been sending packages.

As they were driving through the city, they came upon a tollgate. Sammy was excited and very impressed about all the new sights he was seeing... As they pulled up to the tollgate and the collector reached out for the money, Sammy wanted to know what was happening. They told him that he was a toll collector.

"What a wonderful way to earn money," Sammy said in German. The Lesters found it amusing, but also poignant. It gave them a fresh perspective of life in the big city compared to the kind of life that Sammy must have led this far in war-torn Europe.

Sammy and Sara lived in the temporary home in New York City for a couple of weeks. They were interviewed by the committee members. All the children were trying to learn English quickly. After all, this was to be their new home. Sammy wanted to learn as much as possible as soon as possible about the new country, the new language and the new customs.

The case material about Sammy and Sara read:

> *I was immediately impressed by these two children who were younger than most of the other children arriving in their group. They are good-looking, alert and unusually well-mannered.*
>
> *Sammy is a handsome child, young looking for his age. He proudly used the little English he had learned. I was amazed to learn that he had studied it for only two weeks since he had not known definitely before that time that he would be coming to America.*
>
> *Sammy said that he hoped he would be placed with a family as soon as possible so that he could begin his studies.*

Eventually the two children were taken to a foster home on Marquette Street in Chicago by the Jewish Children's Bureau, an agency of the Jewish Federation of Chicago. Again, it was to be a temporary placement for the children while waiting to be adopted. The family with whom they were placed had two daughters. Sammy started school and began to learn English in earnest. He also learned how to catch a baseball and how to play football. There were lots of new challenges. It was quite demanding to be learning so many new things, but also quite exciting. The food was good. The people were nice. It was fabulous.

Rosa wrote long letters in German to Sammy and Sara. Sammy was quite good about writing back every week. He was telling her about all he was learning and experiencing.

Eventually Sammy and Sara were taken by a social worker to several homes to visit prospective parents. The social workers were having trouble finding a home that would take both children. A wonderful family was found for Sara on Chicago's South Side.

Sara continured her education and eventually married and had three sons. Sam and Sara continued to see each other even though distance separated them.

One day Sammy was taken to meet some people from Northbrook, a northern suburb of Chicago.

> *I was introduced to a woman in a Buick with a nice little girl. I couldn't speak English much yet, so I was quite quiet as we went to lunch. I didn't know what to order, as I couldn't read English, so I let them order for me. They loved me and I loved them.*

Sammy thought this woman was the most beautiful, warm woman he had ever seen. She was wearing white gloves, and her daughter was a bouncy little eight year old girl with two front teeth missing.

After lunch, they all drove what seemed a long way into the country. They came to a dusty little lane that was full of holes. It was quiet and peaceful as they drove up this very woody lane.

The sky was blue and the sun was shining. A little white and brown dog with long ears barked as he greeted us at the car. He sniffed, then jumped on me with his front paws and licked my hands with his long tongue. That was Jimmy, my dog-to-be.

Another car drove up the lane. A distinguished-looking man with a mustache, wearing a business suit got out of the car. He put out his hand to greet the boy. Sammy, told that the man was a pediatrician, tried to impress him by saying in broken English, that he wished to become a doctor someday himself. The man smiled.

We walked around the beautiful grounds. Many tall yellow daffodils were blooming in the wooded lot next to a dense forest. Other spring flowers were beginning to bloom. The air was cool and crisp. I was walking with my new dad, trying to stand tall and pretending to understand what he was saying. I walked around my new home. It was a piece of heaven.

Sammy was led to the warmth of his beautiful new home, the home of Dr. Ellis Harris, his wife Harriet Golden Harris, and their daughter, Sue Harris. They showed Sammy his room—a room of his very own! It had two windows. The window on the north was touched by leaves from a tall tree.

This was Sammy's new home, a home and family which welcomed him with love and warmth and accepted him immediately. Sammy, now twelve and a half years old, was finally home.

> *There was a new peace in my soul. To have a room of my own for the first time in my life. To have a mother and father who would love me and whom I would love. To have a new little sister who would say with pride, "This is my big brother!" This was the beginning of life, my life, my new life as Samuel Rzeznik Harris, son of Dr. and Mrs. Ellis Harris. I was like other children at last.*

Sam immediately began to adapt to his new life. He put away his old life, including his old name of Sammy, as if packing it away.

Mrs. Harris wrote to a social worker:

> *Sam came to live with us on April 10, 1948. Along with his personal belongings he brought with him a pair of white mice for which he had great enthusiasm. He unpacked his clothing with dispatch, showed us his few treasures and pictures brought from*

71

Europe, gave to Susan little things he said he didn't want, and when he was finished, gave me his two suitcases with instructions to throw them out because he never wanted to see them again. He definitely was locking the door to his past.

And Sam did lock the door to his past. It was almost as if he instinctively knew that in order to live in this wondrous future he had been offered, he would have to give up the past. He locked the door to the painful memories of the skinny deprived child who had been starving in the concentration camps, and he threw away the key.

Above left: Sam and Sara
(on right) in 1945 with
an unidentified friend.
Above: Sam and Sara, 1948.
Left: Rosa 1948.

Chapter Twelve
Becoming Whole Again

Sam was placed in sixth grade in Crestwood School in Northbrook, Illinois. He participated in many activities, but one of his favorites was the Boy Scouts. After two years in scouting, he became a Life Scout. That achievement made him feel quite accomplished.

He became a leader in his school. His parents were very proud of him when he was picked from among all of his classmates to receive the coveted American Legion Award upon graduation.

Sam went on to an excellent-rated high school, New Trier, in Winnetka, Illinois. He found a whole world of possibilities opened up to him.

I took advantage of everything the school had to offer. I played football, baseball, and became a wrestler. I studied dramatics and was in a few plays. I was elected to student council, and then president of my class. I felt that I was well on my way to my goals when I graduated in 1954.

After graduating from Grinnell College in 1958 in Grinnell, Iowa, Sam went on to become a leader in his community. He excelled in everything he did, and was well-liked by everyone. His natural way with people helped him succeed in business. Soon he was winning awards right and left.

He became active in community and scholastic affairs, serving on the boards of Spertus College, Forest Hospital, and South Central Bank, and he was very active in the Rotary Club. He was President of the Northbrook United Way, a Commissioner of the Boy Scouts of America for the northern suburbs of Chicago and Vice President of the local chapter of B'nai Brith.

In business, he rose quickly in the ranks of the Equitable Life Assurance Company where he served as agent until his promotion to District Manager and eventually Agency Manager. He became a life member of the Million Dollar Round Table and qualified for the exclusive Equitable Hall of Fame.

His family life was equally successful. He had married a beautiful and talented woman, Dede, and they raised two wonderful children, David and Julie.

Still, he did not talk about the little boy Sammy that he had been in Poland. He had locked that part away, put it in a compartment and left it there.

Dede, being the loving wife that she was, realized something was not quite right. She had studied psychology and social work at the University of Chicago, and she felt that in spite of all of Sam's success, something was missing.

One chilly Chicago weekend, Dede and Sam were warming themselves by their fireplace. It was a cozy evening, the kind that invites intimacy. Dede started asking Sam about "little Sammy."

"What is it about little Sammy that you dislike?" she asked.

"That little boy is ugly. He has ripped clothing. He was skinny and starving!" Sam replied.

"Let's talk about that little boy," Dede prodded. "Was he brave?"

"He must have been brave," admitted Sam. "He didn't give up. He was fighting all these things, and he survived."

"Can you be proud of that little boy?" she asked.

"Yes, I can be proud," said Sam with a little grin. He was getting the idea that Dede was sneaking into his head. Yes, that little Sammy might have been skinny and starving and had rags around his feet, but that little Sammy had a lot of strength and character. It was that Sammy who made it possible for the adult Sam to achieve a happy, successful life. So little Sammy was someone to be proud of.

From that moment on, Sam began to reconnect with the Sammy in his life. The part of him he had split off became part of him again. He became whole.

He had locked part of himself away in order to survive the new life he had been given because the past would destroy him if he dwelled in it. Now it was time to reconnect the past and the present in order to help the world with the future.

That wholeness made Sam aware of what his responsibility was concerning his past. He realized he wanted his children to know that hate was wrong, and could lead to terrible things such as what he had experienced. At the same time, he wanted them to know that in spite of bad things in the world, people were basically good and that we should find the good in them and love them.

Sam and Dede took their children to Israel, and then went on to visit Europe. Sam insisted they visit Germany, because he wanted his children to learn not to hate the German people. He told them they could despise Hitler, but not the Germans. He wanted to free them of the burden of hate.

The World Gathering of Holocaust Survivors in Jerusalem was planned for 1981. Dede said to Sam, "Honey, wouldn't it be wonderful if we went with our children?"

Sam said no. She asked why not. He just said he didn't want to go.

Dede, being the gentle but persistent person she is, said a week later, "Honey, it will be wonderful for our whole family to march with the survivors through the streets of Jerusalem to the Wailing Wall."

Again, Sam said no.

Later, I asked myself why I was resisting so much. It occurred to me that I was getting the shivers every time the subject came up. The thought of marching with my fellow survivors again was very frightening. The last time I marched with these people was indelibly imprinted on my mind. I remembered the Nazis with helmets and bayonetted guns coming to my town of Deblin in Poland and forcing the Jews out of their homes. They lined them up and marched them off into cattle cars that took them to one of the concentration camps. Most of the members of my family were in those lines. I was in those lines. I did not want to go again—it was too emotional for me.

Eventually, Sam did decide to go to the world reunion. He realized the trip would have a lasting impact on the entire family, in spite of any bad memories that he might have. He also decided that with his luck, everything would be all right.

Six thousand survivors attended the meeting. Daily busses took them to a meeting place called the Survivors' Village. One day, tired of waiting for the bus, Sam and his family took a cab. They invited an elderly couple to join them to share the ride.

The man asked what country and camp I came from. I told him that I came from Poland and that I was in two camps, Deblin and Czestochowa. I said that no one here would know me because I was a child and had hidden under beds in the camps.

Upon hearing this, the man gasped, "I was in Czestochowa!" and he began to sob. His wife, whose concentration numbers were visible to me, also began to cry. This man, with tears running down his cheeks, turned to my children and said, "Your father is a very lucky man—you should only know how lucky he is!"

Dede asked him to tell us.

He began to calm down and told us about my luck and his pain. He told us how he had to take the children, put them in a truck take them from the camp and deliver them to the Nazis outside the camp, where the Nazis would shoot them. Many of the children were tortured first by being picked up by the hair and thrown in the air. He remembered how he was to do the same with five more children who somehow were spared. I was one of those children. He could never forgive himself for performing those horrors.

They remembered more. Sam remembered how he entered the camp through the barbed wire gates, how the Jewish people hugged and kissed him and passed him from hand to hand above their heads, and how each was so happy to see a child again. The gentleman said that these people had not seen a child in two years.

We spoke of other things and when I remembered them, he cried and we hugged—a confirmation for both of us that these things were not nightmares, that they were all realities which we brought with us from different corners of the world.

This gathering was very therapeutic for me. It proved to me and my family that my past is just what I told them it was.

This meeting was a gathering of the toughest people on earth. There was no pity displayed, only great pride. It is a miracle when one thinks that thirty-six years ago each person had to fight off nightmares, get accustomed to being without loved ones, learn to live in new lands, learn new professions, and build a new family while not wasting too much time dwelling on the past. We had to learn to love and be loved, to forgive, and to build for the future.

I am proud of my fellow survivors and all the people of our great State of Israel for the tremendous accomplishments of building and piecing together their own lives and, at the same time, building a country miraculously out of sand. As a Jew, I never felt more free and proud than I did at that moment. The dignity shown there proves that there is great hope for the Jewish people and possibly for the whole world.

SAMMY: *Child Survivor of the Holocaust*

In 1985, Sam went to Philadelphia to attend an American gathering of Holocaust survivors, and was interviewed by *U.S. News and World Report* (May 6). Sam was quoted as saying, "I was nine and a half when I was liberated. America made everything possible for me. I wrestled in high school and college, played football and baseball. I was an American kid. It was easy for me to forget, and I did for 40 years. But I really care that it should not happen to other children—Jewish, black or Christian. Democracy is the only thing that can help us prevent it. When I went to Philadelphia, I went to mourn the deaths of six million—but also to celebrate for those of us who are alive. I feel we outwitted the evil that always tries to win over good but never seems to in the long run. If any SS are still around—tell them I'm here, I'm happy."

Sam's new American sister, Sue, had heard little about the details of his childhood in Poland. When the *U.S. News and World Report* article was about to be published, he decided it was time to talk to her about it. He went to visit her in her home near Chicago, and said, "Sue, we need to talk. You know a little bit about my first years in Poland, but I didn't talk about it while growing up in Northbrook. Well, now I'm talking about it again, and I wanted you to know before the rest of the world knows."

Sam and Sue discussed his past for a couple of hours, with Sam filling her in on the part of his life he had hidden for so many years.

Then he asked, "Why didn't you ever ask about it?"

Emotionally moved, she said, "Because you were my brother."

She had accepted him completely as he was, her new brother, and nothing else mattered to her. Now that he was willing to discuss the hidden past, they could still be close as brother and sister, but he no longer felt the need to hide that part of himself.

Sam began speaking in schools and organizations about his past. He knew that by letting people know what he had been through as a child in the concentration camps, he could inspire people and make them understand that life has its difficulties, but those difficulties can be overcome. Life is good if we let it be.

Sam's message has been very clear: hate is pointless. Love is good. Your life can be good. You have the means to make it be a good life. He continues to spread this message to people around the world.

Dr. Ellis and Harriet Golden Harris.

Sister Sue and Sam, 1948.

Above: The Harris
home in Northbrook, IL.
Right: Jimmy, the
Harris family dog.

Chapter Thirteen
Return to Poland
(54 Years Later)

The last time I saw my hometown of Deblin, Poland was January 1945, when I was nine and a half, right after the Russian Army liberated us. After the war I had made it a point not to look at a map of my town or the country of Poland. I wanted to erase the location from my mind.

In June 1999, my wife Dede encouraged me to visit Poland and to face my past. I had all kinds of strange feelings and fears when I thought of stepping on the ground where my family suffered and died.

On June 27,1999, I wrote the following in my diary:

> *I am on the Polish Lot Air Line with my wife Dede. We are on the way to Warsaw, Poland and we will be there in four hours. It has been several months now since I made the decision to face my past. I must*

85

admit that they have not been easy days and weeks. The Holocaust and all the atrocities keep flashing through my mind. I have lost sleep, I have had many bad dreams and even cried secretly. My wife and children must know intuitively that this is difficult on me even though I try not to show my emotions. I told them that I am tough and can handle those horrible memories of the past.

I am looking out of the window of the airplane and see dark clouds floating by, thousands of feet beneath. My brain feels as though it has a abscess on it. By going to Deblin the abscess will be lanced. It will be painful. My concern is how and if the raw wound will heal. Will it get more infected? I think, my positive mental attitude and support of my loving wife will help me heal.

We landed in Warsaw pretty much on time. Our Polish guide, George, speaking perfect English would be driving us first to my hometown, Deblin, next to my grandparent's village, Czolna and finally to the two concentration camps in which I was hidden for several years.

We were approaching Deblin. I could not believe that I saw a sign, "Deblin, Straight Ahead." I cannot describe all of the emotions that were in my being; sad, nervous, and perhaps curiosity tinged with slight excited anticipation.

In Deblin, George, our guide took us to an antique store where we met the town historian. Mr. Lucinski remembered all that had transpired during the war. He took us to where we lived when I was a child. I still remembered my address—Okolna 25. The house was not there any more. The well in the back yard, from which I drew water was still there. As we stood looking at the street, I smelled something sweet and pleasant. My favorite odor. It was lilac. Dede looked at me, "Now I know why you always plant lilac bushes near our window wherever we live." I too, did not know why I planted so many lilac bushes until that moment.

I told George, "If we walk around the bend there should be a mikvah (ritual bath house). That is where my father took me frequently." We walked around the corner and it was just as I remembered from so many years ago. Now the building had broken windows and bullet holes in it. Looking through the broken windows we saw rubbish and rusty pipes and no indication that it had once been used for sacred purposes.

We continued to walk to the center of the village. I saw the place where the Germans gathered the Jews and beat them to form lines for the final march to the cattle cars. I remarked to Mr. Lucinski, "This is the place where the cattle cars waited. Am I right?" The town historian said, "Yes," with sadness in his voice. The last time I saw my family was when they were marching towards those cattle cars.

I continued, "This is where my father pushed me

87

out of the line and told me to run and hide behind the pile of bricks." Mr. Lucinski confirmed my memory, "Yes," he said, "they were constructing a new building there."

As we approached the Deblin concentration camp, Dede looked at the ground and saw a stone with Hebrew writing on it. We were upset to learn that the sidewalks we were walking on were made of grave stones from Jewish cemeteries.

In the concentration camp, the wooden barracks were collapsed rotten wood. I was able to show Dede approximately where I hid. A factory complex was made from part of the concentration camp, with nothing remodeled or torn down. Everything was there but the inmates. Nothing was marked or preserved to remember.

The whole scene brought me back to the time when I was being bitten by fleas and lice. And even now, mosquitoes from the swampy area located near the Vistula River were ferocious. We agreed to leave immediately. The stone paths to the airport where the exhausted inmates marched to work and the railroad tracks where hundreds of thousands of Jews were transported to Treblinka and Auschwitz were still there.

Back in his antique store, I asked Mr. Lucinski where I might find a Torah, a sample of my father's Hebrew writing, anything that may have been written by my father. He pulled some parchment from his desk drawer and said "This has just been found in the house next to where your family lived. They are just starting to tear down the house and this was found in the attic." He held three pieces of Torah parchment which had rivets on all sides. The parchment was old and worn.

I was so excited. Perhaps my father did write this. There was no way of knowing. No scribe ever signs a Torah. We now have the parchment framed over my desk in my study.

Mr. Lucinski's son had painted a picture of the Deblin Concentration Camp in which he depicts two barracks with a man hung by his neck swinging between the barracks. This explained everything to me. No wonder I wet my bed. Who wouldn't be terrified to pass this body in the black of night while going to the latrine.

Just before we left Deblin, Mr. Lucinski handed us a book he compiled, *Homo Homini, Martyrology of Jews in Deblin,* written in 1987. This book won the Polish History Award. Citizens of Deblin were interviewed and described what they saw during the war. "Shots were fired left and right. Nobody looked at age or gender anymore. They shot everything that moves. There was segregation. Young and healthy were moved to the right, the rest to the left. The rest were the elderly, children, (even the youngest ones in strollers), literally everyone who did not show a promise of squeezing out some more strength for work. Hiding in the recesses of the houses was to no avail. They would be reached by bullets there. And these are peculiar bullets. If someone was hit in the head, the bullet splits the head in half."

"This peculiar segregation lasted until the afternoon. Streets are strewn with dead bodies of children, women and men. The soldiers sent here from the airfield were in Deblin to help the police, shoot and murder evicted Jews with bayonets. One of them stabbed a child in a stroller with a bayonet. He lifted the baby like a sheaf of grain is lifted with the pitchfork, and tossed it to the side. The baby's mother was watching...."

"A Nazi in a green uniform armed with a machine pistol, shot a mother pushing a stroller. The mother was killed on the spot. The soldier walked up to the stroller and fired four shots at the child in the stroller from a distance of one meter. When the soldier walked away, the child was still alive and was not even hurt. Two Polish women ran up, took the child and ran away toward Warszawska Street." All of this and more was going on as I was hiding with my sisters, Rosa and Sara in the hayloft. Once again the horror of my young life was confirmed.

George, our guide, said, "Now we are off to Czestochowa." I remembered being transported from the Deblin concentration camp to Czestochowa in cattle cars pushed together like sardines without water, food or other amenities. I felt victorious, as now I was chauffeured in a limousine to the same destination. I enjoyed the countryside as the fresh air rushed through the open windows. In the distance I saw a field of poppies. The whole field was red from the flowers. I remembered when I was a small boy before the war, I had seen that same scene.

The Czestochowa concentration camp was a disappointment. They had recently destroyed the barracks in which we were packed tightly together. The manager of the factory that had once been a camp, a middle age woman, unlocked the gate and let us in only because I said that I was a survivor from what used to be the concentration camp. She told our guide in Polish that we had it so rough, we were crammed in a small space, beaten, hungry and overworked. She felt so sorry for me.

The train tracks on which we had arrived so many years ago were still there with an old broken down German cattle car which probably was used to transport us. The Nazi insignia was still on the car. There was no indication of what this area had ever been used for, no memorial, no words of respect for those who had suffered or remorse for past actions.

I showed Dede where we got off the train and where they sent me after separating me from my sisters. I was sent to the left to be shot. I was too young to work. At point, I remember being kicked in the chest by an SS soldier.

I pointed out where I was left overnight with four other children waiting to be taken to the woods to be shot.

The only other items I identified were several thick concrete towers which the Nazis used on guard duty. These enormous towers lay on the ground sideways with weeds growing through and around them. I felt good standing tall, healthy and upright next to these fallen towers. I felt that the human spirit had survived the bestiality. We left through the same gate which the Russian Army liberated us on January 17, 1945. What a wonderful feeling that was.

My memories were confirmed. This day I felt great sadness but even greater relief. I had not made all this up. Being so young when all of this happened I had begun to think that perhaps I had exaggerated the horror of it all. No, unfortunately, this had been my reality.

Chapter Fourteen
Cholna
My Grandparents' Farm

Our next stop was the little town of Cholna, where my maternal grandparents had lived. My parents, siblings and I visited them on the Sabbath and on other holidays. We traversed dangerous roads through woods and fields, always with the possibility of being attacked by angry hoodlums. Having no auto, we traveled by horse and buggy. I was always so excited to see my grandparents, Sara and I loved to play by the ponds with the ducks and eat our grandmother's delicious chalah.

Driving through the roads now, I commented to Dede about the contrast in the mode of transportation and the relative safety in which we now traveled. This amazing change had taken place all in one lifetime, my lifetime.

When we came to Cholna, our guide knocked on a farmhouse door from which a ninety-three year old man by the name of Mazurek emerged. Our guide asked in Polish, "Did you know a Liebe Hershman?"

(my grandfather) The old farmer said he had worked at my grandfather's shingle factory on his farm and agreed to take us to my grandparent's farm. As we walked over to their farm I asked, "Can you tell me about Liebe Hershman?" Mr. Mazurek said that the corner we were walking towards was known as Liebe's Corner and that he was "liked by everyone. He was a very good man." Mr Mazurek and my grandfather had been "close friends."

As we were visiting on "Liebe's Corner", a woman walked over to us. She looked about sixty-five years old. She too, remembered my grandparents. Her name is Grzewa. Her father's name was Parzszek. Grzewa remembered going to my grandparents' house on the Sabbath with her father to light the stove. (Orthodox Jews cannot work on the Sabbath. Lighting a stove is considered work. Christian neighbors understood this and cooperated by lighting the stoves for the Jewish people).

Grzewa invited us to her home where we drank orange juice and sang Polish songs we learned as children. Grzewa's many grandchildren looked on.

That night, I slept well. Yes, my wonderful grandparents, I so often remembered, did exist. They lived on in the fond memories of all those who knew them, Jew, Gentile, family and neighbors.

Some day Dede and I hope to return to Cholna with our children and grandchildren.

1999 Visit to Cholna

Mr. Mazurek, grandparents' friend

Grzewa, grandparents' neighbor
with grandchildren, Sam and Dede

Chapter Fifteen
Personal Commitment

After my return from Poland and reliving my concentration camp experiences, it became quite apparent to me that I wanted to devote the rest of my life to memorializing the millions of victims that suffered and perished at the hands of evil. I have been very active in the Illinois Holocaust Museum and Education Center whose missions coincides with my dreams. This is the mission statement.

"The Illinois Holocaust Museum and Education Center is dedicated to the remembrance of the Holocaust (1933-1945) and the furtherance of education about that tragic period and its aftermath. The Center carries out its mission through the exhibition, preservation and interpretation of its collected artifacts, and through a broad spectrum, of educational services and resources. The primary goal of the Center is to enhance awareness of the universal lessons of the Holocaust by teaching the consequences of hatred and prejudice, and to foster an understanding that differences among people are to be cherished, rather than feared."

We currently have a small, overcrowded museum of less than 5,000 square feet. Unfortunately, as events teach us every day, the need to fight hatred extends far beyond what we can accomodate in that small space. Each year more than 2.4 million children attend primary and secondary schools in Illinios, yet our current facility can only reach 25,000. If we are to reach significantly more of our region's students and adults, we must have a much larger museum and dramatically expanded programming effort.

Given this crucial need, I volunteered to be the Chairperson of the committee spearheading development and construction of a new 50,000 square foot facility to be located in Skokie, Illinois. The Board of Directors also recently elected me President of Foundation. Our organization has a dedicated group of survivors and other volunteers from all walks of life who are working day and night to fulfill this mission.

In developing our new facility, we have been blessed with some of the most talented designers in the world. Award-winning architect, Stanley Tigerman, has designed a magnificent building which will bring meaning both through its contents and its structure. To help Mr. Tigerman design the interior exhibits, the world's two greatest experts have agreed to collaborate for the first time on our project. Michael Berenbaum has written over a dozen books on the Holocaust and was project director for the U.S. Holocaust Museum in Washington, D.C. Yizhak Mais is the Director of the

Historical Museum at Yad Vashem, Israel's Holocaust Museum. Working together they have brought life to our vision.

Year-round, our Foundation gets requests from schools and other groups to have a member of our Speaker's Bureau speak about their Holocaust experiences. It is emotionally draining and forever memorable for both the students and the survivor.

Recently, I was invited to speak in front of one hundred and fifty students and fifteen teachers in a school in Highland Park, Illinois. I was told they had already been studying the Holocaust for a couple of weeks and was impressed with their penetrating questions. Just before the school bell rang, a teacher in the back of the room asked a question no one had ever expressed: "Mr. Harris, of the hour and a half we have been together, what one thing would you like the children to carry away with them?" Without hesitation, I said:

> *I arrived here early this morning and noticed your beautiful playgrounds. On those playgrounds you will see bullies pushing other children around. Hitler was one of the worst bullies. Just as we watch idly by in the playground, we also watched Hitler. We must stop the bullies. We cannot watch and do nothing. Doing nothing is doing something.*

The class ended with all the teachers giving me thumbs-up while the students applauded.

Two days later, I answered the phone in my home. It was Nancy, the seventh grade student reporter who was writing a story about my visit. She said, "Mr. Harris, it worked! It worked! Three of us saw a bully in the playground and we stopped him!" these children got the message and acted. The rest of the world must do the same.

As long as I am able, I shall continue to bear witness to the reality that unchecked bigotry and hatred can lead to the most heinous crimes conceivable by man, but that through our actions, we can make a difference. Yet, I know I cannot live forever It is impreative that these lessons continue to be taught long after my generation of survivors has passed from this world.

With the support we have received, I am comforted by the knowledge that our new museum and education center can and will continue to make a meaningful difference in the lives of our world for generations to come. It is my legacy and the legacy of all survivors everywhere.

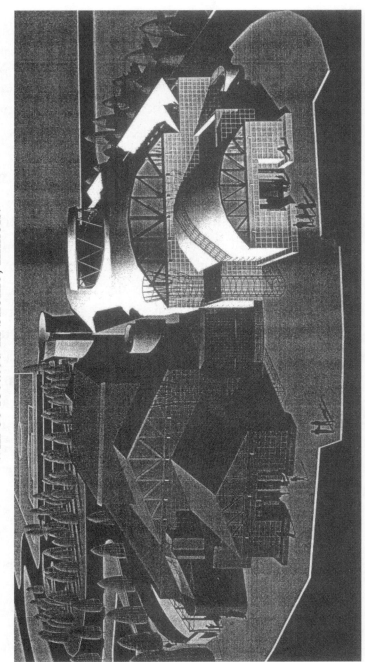

The future Holocaust Museum and Education Center of Illinois will be located in Skokie, Illinois.

Architect: Stanley Tigerman

Epilogue

Sam's sister, Rosa, continues to live in Vienna. Walter died a few years ago, but she still has her two sons, Herman and Jackie, and two grandchildren.

In 1965, Sam and Dede brought Rosa, Herman, and Jackie to live in Chicago so they could have a better life in America. Rosa tried very hard to learn the customs and the language in the United States, but life had taken its toll on her. She decided going back to Vienna was much easier for her. Rosa does come back to the United States for weddings and important events. Sam and Dede visit her in Vienna whenever possible.

Sara and her husband, Herb, live in the suburbs of Chicago and have three children and five grandchildren.

Sam and Dede live in the suburbs of Chicago near their children, David and Julie and Julie's husband, Jeff, and their children Jeremy and Jessica.

Dr. and Mrs. Ellis Harris are both deceased. Sam's sister, Sue, lives in the northern suburbs of Chicago.

Samuel R. Harris is a very inspirational speaker

who is often invited to speak to large audiences, such as grade schools, high schools, Rotary meetings, Holocaust survivor groups, and many more. He appeared in April, 1999 at a national Holocaust Memorial Observance Program sponsored by the U.S. Social Security Administration in Baltimore, Maryland. Sam is currently President of the Illinois Holocaust Memorial Foundation.

In the Appendix are copies of letters that school children and community leaders have written to Sam in appreciation for sharing his life experiences. Many people have found his inspiration helps them realize what a good life they have and makes them truly more appreciative of life.

The Holocaust is something that needs to be remembered so this kind of crime against mankind can never happen again. Revisionists are now denying the Holocaust in hundreds of web sites and books. One of Sam's missions in sharing his story with as many people as possible is to help people connect with the reality of the Holocaust. As a Woodstock, Illinois High School student told him, "I will never forget you and your experience. I will pass it on to my children."

Listening to survivors helps people realize that each of the six million Jews who were slaughtered had a story to tell, but they aren't alive to tell it. People like Sam speak for them. Elie Wiesel, Nobel Laureate and famous Holocaust survivor said, "The essence of this tragedy is that it can never be fully conveyed."

People survived through sheer will to live, unwilling to be broken by the oppression of the Nazis. The fact that they survived is a true testament to the human spirit.

Sammy was like a leaf caught in a violent storm, blown from place to place. Each time the winds blew him to the ground, he was touched by special human beings who gave of themselves and helped him. He was blessed with good luck, and I will always believe, the protection of a guardian angel. The luck, the angel, and the wonderful people spurred Sammy on to survive.

I, Sam, am very thankful to all who helped me become the man I am today—dedicated to people and to life. Because of them, I am happy.

Sam with sisters, Rosa and Sara

Good will prevail in the long run.

Sam's Family, 2004

Son David, Sam and Dede, grandchildren Jessica, Jeremy, daughter Julie & son-in-law Jeff.

Letters

This section contains a representation of the many letters received from people thanking him for his inspirational messages.

THE WHITE HOUSE

WASHINGTON

July 12, 1999

PERSONAL

Mr. Samuel R. Harris
98 Manchester Drive
Buffalo Grove, Illinois   60089

Dear Sam:

Ken Apfel passed along your thoughtful letter and
the signed copy of your book. I'm pleased to have
them and to know that you were able to participate
in the Holocaust Memorial Observance program, and
I understand that you conveyed a powerful message.
I look forward to reading your account of your
wartime experiences. Your story sounds both
moving and inspiring.

There will one day come a time when the Holocaust
will pass from living reality and shared experience
to memory and history, and each of us has a solemn
obligation to ensure that this tragedy is never
forgotten. By sharing your personal story, you
are helping the world heed the lessons of history,
and I thank you for speaking out.

Hillary and I send our best wishes.

Sincerely,

Bill Clinton

Letter from President Clinton

107

S T E V E N   S P I E L B E R G

April 29, 2004

Dear Samuel,

I am thrilled to tell you that 2004 marks the 10th anniversary of Survivors of the Shoah Visual History Foundation. These have been exciting, productive, and wondrous years. In 1994, I could not fully foresee the power, impact, and success of this massive archive, or how your testimony and the 52,000 others we have collected would ultimately affect those who watch them. But survivors convinced me that their stories, your story, had to be told.

Today, I am honored to tell you that young people and adults are watching your testimonies in schools, libraries, museums, and universities—not only in the United States, but in countries around the world. Through documentaries, special collections, educational products and programs, and as research tools for scholars and researchers, your testimonies are making a profound difference by creating a bridge between history and contemporary issues.

It is thanks to you, and your willingness to recall, retell, and record testimony, that all this is possible. The archive will serve as a valuable resource not only for countless people today, but for future generations. It is through your generosity that children 100 years from now and beyond will hear and learn about the terrible consequences of hatred and racism. By hearing your voice and seeing your face, they will recognize that they have the power to bring about change and act against intolerance.

I want to thank you so very much for your priceless contribution to the Shoah Foundation archive. You are helping us to achieve our urgent mission to overcome prejudice, intolerance, and bigotry — and the suffering they cause — through the educational use of the Foundation's visual history testimonies.

I am proud of what we have accomplished together, and you have made it possible. I thank you for your priceless gift.

All my best,

Steve

SURVIVORS OF THE SHOAH VISUAL HISTORY FOUNDATION · POST OFFICE BOX 3168 · LOS ANGELES, CA 90078-3168

Letter from Steven Spielberg

Dear Mr. Harris

    I am very thankful that you came to our school, to tell us of the hardships, of World War II. I was really not sure of the cruelty, before you came, but now I know. Thanks to you, one of the youngest holocaust survivors, the truth can be told from generation, to generation, and it will never be changed.

Sincerely,

Letter from a student.

Dear Mr. Harris,

My name is   I am amazed by
what you went through and survived. The majority of kids
probably would have not been able to handle something
like that. I know that you probably receive hundreds of
letters like this, but I am continually amazed that you
survived and staved off clinical depression, as I need thirty
milligrams of Prozac a day to get along. You had shown a
strong will to live through the worst of times, in such
gravity of peril that is incomparable to anything in the
twentieth century. To me the criminal acts of genocide
enacted by the Nazis are not only unthinkable, but also
unspeakable. Government officials are afraid to take this
diplomatic tiger by the tail and show everyone that it *did*
happen and people *died* at those camps, just to remove all
confusion caused by crackpots who say that the holocaust
did not happen. The result is that people are growing
complacent and detached, which is inviting such acts to
occur again. You are doing something noble and
important… reinforcing the knowledge in people's minds
that it *really happened* and that these were people, not a
story.

Signed,

Letter from a student.

SAMMY: Child Survivor of the Holocaust

May 13, 2002

Dear Mr. Harris,

My name is _____ I attend Woodstock High School. I am a 9th grader. I listened to you share your most frightful and most sad feelings about your childhood with us. I admire you greatly for that. I want to thank you for being willing to bring back all the bad memories of your childhood experiences. Any other person would have not talk about that and would have rather tried to leave the past behind them.

Your speech made me understand how horrible Jews were treated. Before you came to share your feelings with us, I did not think much about the Holocaust. I just knew that many Jews had died but that was all. Now I know that the Holocaust was an act of racism. Although the Holocaust has been over for a long time, racism is still seen today. Not only towards Jews but other people from different back rounds too. My parents are Mexican, but I was born here in the U.S. For me being from a different back round makes me different. I am also sometimes faced with discrimination and racism. I share with you the same feelings about that horrible incident from the past that took your family and identity away from you. I understand how much you hate Hitler and despise racism. I wish that someday in the future, racism will not be seen anymore. I hope that one day people will look back and talk about racism as just a bad nightmare. To me everyone is the same, we all have different physical appearance but what really matters is what people have in the inside.

People like you are the type of people who make a difference in life. Thank you again for taking the time to come down to Woodstock High. Most of all thank you for being willing to bring back all you bad nightmares just give us a better perspective of the Holocaust.

Sincerely,

Letter from a student.

111

Dear Mr. Harris

I can't tell you how much I learned from you when you came to Woodstock High School. I think that this is a priceless gift of knowledge you share with the kids learning about the holocaust. When I was hearing about how much you like our school and how many years you have been doing this I was very grateful and amazed. The stories that were told at the start of your part of the presentation I could almost see in my mind what was going on. But I will never know what it was really like. Only you and the others like you that had to put up with all of the pain and suffering would know. But because of you I have a better idea of what was going on. It makes me disgusted, sad, and mad at the people who think that the holocaust was never real. I am looking forward to reading your book. I hope you are able to tell more people about what went on and tell them you stories. I still would never have the strength to go through horrible dreams before and after just so I could tell some one something. This shows how much dedication, and determination you have. I hope that you will keep coming back to our school and tell other students what had happened. After I saw you and heard what happened to you I know I can stand up to any thing or face any thing because you had made it through a even harder situation

                    Sincerely yours,

Letter from a student.

Glossary

Antisemitism   Hostility, prejudice or discrimination against Jewish people or Judaism. The word "Semitic" refers to the descendents of Shem, a common ancestor of Middle Eastern people, but it is now commonly used to refer to Jews.

Auschwitz   The well-known and largest Nazi death camp that was located in Poland near Krakow.

Babushka   Polish word for scarf.

Bar Mitzvah (Also Bat Mitzvah)   A Bar Mitzvah refers to a Jewish boy of the age of 13, and a Bat Mitzvah refers to a Jewish girl of the age of 13. These phrases refer to the coming of age of a Jewish boy or girl. A Jewish child automatically becomes a Bar Mitzvah upon reaching the age of thirteen, and no ceremony is needed to confer these rights and obligations; however the formal ceremony that often accompanies this coming-of-age is very popular. The celebrant participates in the Sabbath services in various ways, such as reciting a blessing, reciting a chant, or reading the entire weekly Torah portion, or leading a prayer. In addition, the ceremony also may include an elaborate reception.

Cheder   A school for Jewish children.

Chalah Traditional braided bread served on Sabbath.

Cholent A traditional slow-cooked stew of beef, beans and barley to be served on Sabbath.

Concentration camp A place to confine large numbers of people. In World War II these camps were places of torture and slaughter of the prisoners.

Crematorium An oven or furnace where people were burned.

Death Camp Camps were the prisoners were placed to be exterminated, such as Treblinka.

Dysentery A disease that plagued people in the concentration camps. This disease is very contagious. Its symptoms are severe diarrhea and stomach cramping.

Extermination Camp Another term for death camp, a place where prisoners were held until they were killed. These camps conducted assembly line slaughters.

Four Questions Traditional questions asked at the Passover Holiday.

Gas Chamber Buildings used to exterminate people during WWII. These buildings had sealed chambers that released poisonous gas used to kill large numbers of people. The main gas used was carbon monoxide, although Auschwitz used Zyklon B.

Genocide The systematic extermination of an entire race, national, ethnic or political group. Comes from the roots *geno* (race) and *cide* (to kill).

Ghetto Area of a city that was partitioned off, usually by fences of barbed wire or brick walls, and which the Jews could not leave without permission.

Hebrew The language of the Torah, the religious scripture of the Jews and the current language of the state of Israel.

Holocaust The mass slaughter of European civilians, especially Jews, by the Nazis in World War II. See "Historical Information."

Israel A state created for the Jewish people following the Holocaust. Formerly known as Palestine.

Jewish Badge The sign which the Jews were required by the Nazis to wear on their clothing. This was usually the Star of David, which is a symbol of Judaism.

Jews The followers of Judaism, the religion of the ancient Israelites from the twelve tribes descended from Jacob. This religion holds that there is one God. Their beliefs are found in the Torah. The first five books of the Hebrew Bible (also called the Old Testament).

Labor Camp   Camps where prisoners were forced to work for the military or government.

Matzah   Unleavened bread traditionally served during Passover.

Palestine   A territory of land that after World War II became Israel and Jordan.

Partisans   Groups of people who escaped either the ghettos or the concentration camps and lived in the woods. They were subject to constant attacks by armed German units and to betrayal by local people. They were also subject to climatic conditions such as bitter cold, and had no medical care or regular food provisions.

Passover   One of the major Jewish religious festivals of the year. It is related to the Exodus from Egypt after generations of enslavement, and is referred to in the book of Exodus. The word refers to the fact that G-d "passed over" the houses of the Jews when He was slaying the firstborn of the houses of Egypt. For this festival, the Jewish people have many symbolic rituals. One is the removal of leaven, which causes bread to rise. Unleavened bread (matzah) made from flour and water is cooked very quickly. This is symbolic of the Jews leaving Egypt very quickly and not having time to let the bread rise with leaven. Passover lasts for seven days (eight days outside Israel). On the first and last day, no work is allowed.

Pogrom   Attacks on Jews by non-Jews that occurred for centuries in Europe.

Sabbath (Shabbat) The Jewish day of rest and spiritual enrichment.   Orthodox Jewish people (who abide by the strictest traditional rules) do no work whatsoever on the Sabbath. In the prewar days in Poland, Sabbath was observed so strictly that no lights were turned on (this was considered work) and no travel was allowed.

Scribe The Torah used in services is always written on parchment scrolls. They are always hand-written by a respected person called a scribe. These scrolls are never to be touched by hands. Instead, a pointer in the shape of a hand is used.

Seder   The family home ritual conducted as part of Passover.

Shtetl Yiddish word for small Jewish town or village.

Simchas Torah (Simkhat Torah) A holiday celebrating the completion of the weekly reading of the Torah.

Sobibor   A death camp in which over 250,00 Jews were gassed.

Star of David Symbol of Judaism, a six-pointed star formed by two interlacing triangles, one upside down. Also called the Magen David or the Shield of David.

SAMMY: Child Survivor of the Holocaust

Synagogue Jewish house of worship. Also called a temple.

Torah Refers to the Five Books of Moses: Genesis, Exodus, Leviticus, Numbers and Deuteronomy. Can also refer to the entire Jewish body of scripture and in its broadest sense can refer to the entire body of Jewish law and teachings. The Torah used in services is always written on parchment scrolls. Hand-written by a scribe.

Treblinka An estimated 850,000 Jews were killed in this death camp before it was blown up in 1943. Only 540 people survived this camp.

Warsaw The capital of Poland, which was about forty miles from Deblin.

Yiddish A language used by East European Jews made up of German, Hebrew and Slavic elements.

Children and the Holocaust

The number of children who died in the Holocaust is impossible to know exactly, but it is estimated that there were as many as one and a half million children killed. Of that number, 1.2 million children were Jewish, and the others, Gypsy and handicapped children.

Children were targeted by the Nazis because of their race and religion. They were destroyed when they arrived at the concentration camps because they were not old enough and strong enough to perform labor in the slave camps.

Even before the war, the Jewish children were persecuted at their schools by non-Jews. Classmates would avoid their Jewish classmates or be hostile to them. Non-Jewish children were taught that Jewish children were unclean and inferior, and should be avoided. The number of Jewish children in schools was restricted.

Jewish teenagers could not belong to the same clubs or social organizations as non-Jews, and were banned from using public recreational facilities.

As the Nazi influence increased, methods of exterminating Jewish children were developed. Medical personnel collected information about births which was used to indict potential victims. At first, children were killed at hospitals with overdoses of poison and medications. Handicapped children were targeted as victims. The number of children killed in these wards in early WWII was about five thousand.

Children who were orphaned or homeless were at high risk to be killed. Chances of survival for children was minimal if they had no protective adult. After 1939, children were systematically killed upon arrival at concentration camps or upon their birth within a camp. That any children survived any of these camps at all was one of the miracles of the war.

Historical Information

The Holocaust is generally regarded as the systematic slaughter of not only six million Jews, but also five million others, by the Nazis. That's eleven million people who were killed between 1933 and 1945. Racism and hate caused this slaughter.

The period between 1933 and 1939 saw the Nazis rise to power. The word Nazi is the short term for the National Socialist German Workers Party, which was led by Adolf Hitler. The party ideology was anti-Communist, antisemetic, racist, imperialistic and militaristic.

The Nazis believed that Germans were racially superior and that there was a struggle between them and the "inferior races." Thus, the Nazis wanted to exterminate the groups they believed were inferior and a threat to their survival. Besides Jews, groups such as Gypsies, the handicapped, homosexuals, Jehovah's Witnesses, Catholics, Poles, prisoners of war, and political dissidents were killed for their religious, personal, or political beliefs, or for their personal handicaps. The Nazis considered this their "Final Solution."

In pre-war Poland between 1935 and 1937 there

was widespread violence against the Jews. Jews were attacked in streets, shops were broken and looted. There were separate schools for Jews, so that children would "not be infected with their lower morality." Many Poles felt that Jewish influence was evil.

The Nazis started killing people before the concentration camps opened. The first killings occurred in hospitals and medical wards by lethal injections and poisons. Later, they were killing Jews by shooting them in the streets or fields as they were rounding them up for deportation. Eventually, the Nazis became more organized in their methods and rounded up large numbers of people and shipped them by train to extermination centers such as Treblinka and Auschwitz. In addition, millions of people died in the ghettos and camps from starvation, disease, brutality and torture.

World War II lasted from 1939 to 1945. The first concentration camp opened in January 1933 and lasted until the end of the war, May 8, 1945.

First the Jews were forced into ghettos. This happened in Deblin in April 1940. The first Deblin Deportation was May 1942, and was followed by another in September 1942 and a third in October 1942.

Because of rampant antisemetism in Europe, the Nazis had silent support from the civilians. However, there were groups of brave citizens who did hide Jews from the Nazis, at great risk to themselves. If they were caught hiding Jews, the civilians were subject to death.

Denmark was one nation that saved most of its Jews in a nighttime rescue operation in 1943 by ferrying them secretly to Sweden.

The killing of Jews continued in Poland for more than two years after Germany's surrender. This was strong impetus for an exodus of Jews to other countries, Palestine (Israel) in particular. Between 1944 and 1948, 200,000 European Jews went to Palestine, 1,000 to Britain, 72,000 to US and 16,000 to Canada.

Timeline

January 30, 1933
Adolph Hitler is appointed Reich Chancellor (Prime Minister) of Germany.

March 20, 1933
First concentration camp opens at Dachau, Germany.

October 19, 1933
Germany withdraws from The League of Nations.

November 1938
Kristallnacht—an anti-Jewish Nazi pogrom during which hundreds of synagogues were destroyed and 26,000 Jews were put in concentration camps.

March 15, 1939
Czechoslovakia is occupied by Germany.

September 1, 1939
German army invades Poland. World War II begins.

September 21, 1939
Ghettos established in occupied Poland.

April 9, 1940
German army occupies Denmark and southern Norway.

November 15, 1940
Warsaw ghetto sealed off.

April 6, 1941
German army invades Yugoslavia and Greece.

June 22, 1941
Germany attacks U.S.S.R.

September 28-29, 1941
Nearly 34,000 Jews murdered in the Ukraine.

October 23, 1941
Massacre of 19,000 Odessa Jews.

December 11, 1941
Germany and Italy declare war on the U.S.

March 1, 1942
Extermination begins at Sobibor. By October, 1942, 250,000 Jews had been murdered here.

March 17, 1942
Extermination begins at Belzec.

June 1, 1942
Treblinka extermination begins. 700,000 Jews murdered there by August 1943.

October 4, 1942
All Jews still in concentration camps in Germany are sent to Auschwitz.

April 19, 1943
Warsaw ghetto revolt. Liquidation of Warsaw ghetto.

March 19, 1944
Germany invades Hungary.

May 15, 1944
Deportation of 430,000 Hungarian Jews to Auschwitz begins.

June 6, 1944
Allied invasion of Normandy, D-Day.

October 31, 1944
14,000 Slovakian Jews deported to Auschwitz.

January 17, 1945
Evacuation of Auschwitz, the prisoner's Death March begins.

January 27, 1945
Soviet troops enter Auschwitz.

April 1945
Russian army enters Germany from east, Allied army enters from west.

May 8, 1945
Germany surrenders.

November 1945-October 1946
War crime trials held at Nuremberg, Germany.

SAMMY: Child Survivor of the Holocaust

SAMUEL R. HARRIS' *Sammy: Child Survivor of the Holocaust* is a true story of his childhood and the experiences he survived. As a Grinnell student, he told no one of his early life.

"When I, as a Holocaust survivor, tell of what happened, the brutality is always obvious," Harris says. "It is true that the most horrendous and cruel crimes were perpetrated on the Jewish people and others during the war. I want to remind everyone that not all Germans or Polish or Ukrainians were bad people. There are, and always have been, many people in every nation who are good."

"We should always try to find the good in everyone, to find ways to love and not to hate, that is the message of my story."

Harris is retired from the insurance industry and lives with his wife Dede in the Chicago suburbs, near their children and grandchildren. Dede has written a teacher's guide and workbook to accompany *Sammy.*